About
Projective Verse

Postmodern poetics begins with Olson's seminal essay "Projective Verse," and this urgent and remarkable statement of poetics continues to influence new generations of poets with its bold, dynamic, and energetic rush of provocative ideas about how a poet lives and writes in a postmodern world.

—John Faulise

I first read "Projective Verse" in 1962 when I was introduced to Swinburne and realized why everything I'd been taught made it impossible for me to understand either his poetry or his poetics. Both Olson and Swinburne considered poetry as primarily an expressive event in an animate world: spoken and heard voicings, performed and reperformed rather than mused and overheard. From that point all my work on poetry and poetics began to shift. The Modernist poetry that shaped my attentions pivoted around Crane, Moore, Pound, and Williams, and Romanticism/post-Romanticism around Blake, Byron, Poe, and Lautréamont. And soon then came new worlds of addressive voicings out of Ethnopoetics and L=A=N=G=U=A=G=E. Behind all that for me was a chance encounter with an odd couple, Olson and Swinburne. In a word, provocative.

—Jerome McGann

CHARLES OLSON

Projective Verse

75TH ANNIVERSARY EDITION

EDITED BY

George Quasha
& Michael Boughn

CONTRIBUTIONS BY

Ammiel Alcalay, Michael Boughn,
Robert Kelly, Miriam Nichols,
Ed Sanders & Charles Stein

Station Hill Press

BARRYTOWN, NY

Published by Station Hill Press, the publishing project of the Institute for Publishing Arts, Inc., 120 Station Hill Road, Barrytown, NY 12507, a not-for-profit, Federally tax-exempt organization [501(c)(3)].

Online catalogue: www.stationhill.org
E-mail: publishers@stationhill.org

Acknowledgements
Special contribution and support from André Spears and Anne Rosēn. Thanks to Michael Boughn for obtaining rights to "Projective Verse" and the idea of a 75th anniversary edition. We also wish to thank Alana Siegel for her editorial work on this book.

Cover and text design: Susan Quasha

P. 29: Totem Press edition (1955) cover drawing by matsumi kanemitsu.
P. 30: Title page from Totem Press edition (1955).

Library of Congress Catalog Card Number: 2025951453
ISBN: 978-1-58177-241-8

Land Acknowledgment
In the spirit of truth and equity, it is with gratitude and humility that we acknowledge that the Institute for Publishing Arts, Inc. and Station Hill Press reside on the sacred homelands of the Munsee and Muhheaconneok people, who are the original stewards of this land. Today, due to forced removal, the community resides in Northeast Wisconsin and is known as the Stockbridge-Munsee Community.

Contents

Foreword

ED SANDERS

The 75th Anniversary Publication of Projective Verse

Charles Olson wrote "Projective Verse" in 1950, just before writing the first *Maximus Poems*. The initial typed draft of "Projective Verse," dated February 9, 1950, began with:

PROJECTIVE VERSE

(projectile (prospective (percussive

vs.

> the NON-projective, what we have had, pretty much (outside Pound & Williams), what a French critic calls the "closed," the visual verse, the lyric, if you like, the "personal"....

Olson continued writing this epochal manifesto. He sent it to William Carlos Williams, who urged Olson to contact a young writer named Robert Creeley. Olson did this, beginning over 1000 letters back and forth with Creeley during the next 20 years.

In May of 1950, Olson wrote the first Maximus poem. Then "Projective Verse" was published in *Poetry New York 3* in October, and W. C. Williams placed excerpts from "Projective Verse" in his *Autobiography* and wrote Olson that it was "the most admirable piece of thinking about the poem I have recently, perhaps ever, encountered."

During ensuing years "Projective Verse" charged through the rafters of modern poesy. Don Allen placed it prominently in his epochal anthology, *The New American Poetry* in 1960.

I quoted important paragraphs from it in my 1976 manifesto, "Investigative Poetry." In "The Techniques of Investigative Poetry" section of my proposal, I point to certain brilliant lines in "Projective Poetry" as depicting fully to what I was urging for poesy, that poets should start, at least in parts of their work, to write and describe historical events.

And so Olson's great work inspired my books in verse, such as *1968, a History in Verse; Chekhov, a Biography in Verse; The Poetry and Life of Allen Ginsberg;* and *America, a History in Verse.* In addition, there were hundreds and thousands of writers in the coming decades who garnered wisdom from "Projective Verse" in the bewildering complexities of the writing of Poetry. May it provide help for centuries, such as Aristotle's *Poetics* does. Hail to it!!!

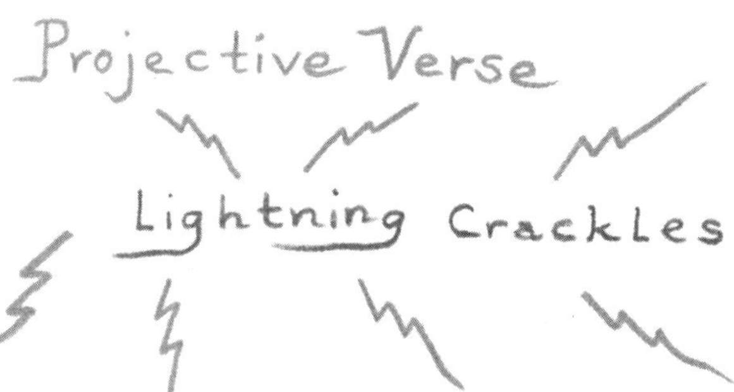

"ONE PERCEPTION MUST IMMEDIATELY AND DIRECTLY LEAD TO A FURTHER PERCEPTION"

and this:

"A poem is energy transferred from where the poet got it, by way of the poem itself to, all the way over to, the reader"

and:

"We now enter.... the large area of the whole poem, into the FIELD.... where all the syllables and all the lines must be managed in their relation to each other."

and this:

"Let me put it baldly. The two halves are:
the HEAD, by way of the EAR, to the SYLLABLE
the HEART, by way of the BREATH, to the LINE"

A Glyph on Inspiring Ideas from **"Projective Verse."**

Preface

MICHAEL BOUGHN

"Resist much. Obey little."
—Walt Whitman

I first read Charles Olson's "Projective Verse" in 1968, a remarkable year whose turbulent energies echoed for me not just in Olson's ideas but in the very syllabic disturbance that animated his language. An illegal, immoral war; revelations of US war crimes; two political assassinations of progressive leaders; the murder of Bobby Hutton (and countless other Black people) by the police; the police/national guard riot in Chicago at the Democratic National Convention; the near overthrow of the French government by students and workers; these all contributed to the creative turbulence of the moment. Many of the extraordinary events of that year circled around growing international opposition to USAmerica's stumbling war against Viet Nam. Student uprisings and massive anti-war street protests were part of it, as was the growing militancy of Black resistance to endemic white (state) racist violence against Black people. Along with that, the work of many artists and poets was dedicated to breaking down aesthetic barriers to the truth, inventing new forms, new modes of creation that challenged the political status quo and the cultural complacencies that accompanied and enabled it. It was a moment of deep temporal disturbance, an outpouring of creative energy that resonated with Bob Dylan's announcement in 1965 regarding termination of his employment on Maggie's Farm. The resistance was spreading, and Olson's essay was very much part of that.

"Projective Verse" was first published in *Poetry New York* 3 in 1950, 75 years ago. At that time, the advances of the modernism of Williams, H.D., Stein, Loy, Pound, cummings and others had been jettisoned or petrified into an Eliotic formalism that provided material for New Critical formal analysis but did nothing to address the shift in our understanding and experience of reality or to realize poetry's visionary soul. Olson's essay blew open the whole scene. He had been working on it for a year, more or less, while corresponding with Frances Boldereff and Robert Creeley, both of whom enthusiastically supported and contributed to his thinking. Five years later, Amiri Baraka/Leroi Jones republished the essay as a pamphlet from his Totem Press, adding to it a letter Olson had written to Elaine Feinstein in response to her correspondence with him.

It's difficult to emphasize how radical "Projective Verse" was in 1950, especially in relation to a poetry world dominated by academic legions in thrall to T.S. Eliot's poetry and criticism. It brought Olson's thinking increased attention. But it wasn't until 1960 when Donald Allen included it prominently in the poetics section of *New American Poetry 1945-1960* that Olson's thinking became front and center in the turbulent contested (re)thinking of poetry's vocation and formal possibility then raging. William Carlos Williams's decision to reproduce two pages of it in his autobiography reinforced Olson's role as spokesman for an insurgent generation of writers.

USAmerican poetry was going through a transition in 1955. Establishment poets, which meant mostly those legitimized by academic recognition who dominated the literary Reviews, were well represented in the publisher's lists. John Crowe Ransom, Randall Jarrell, Elizabeth Bishop, Howard Nemerov, W.H. Auden, A.R. Ammons and others all published new books by "legitimate" publishing houses. But at the same time a rebel movement of non-establishment, non-academic *mimeopress* poets, many of whom would later be represented in Allen's anthology, was growing. The mimeo machine, at that time an advanced technology that facilitated mass production of printed material, was ubiquitous in classrooms and businesses. Seizing the means of production, poets across the country began publishing their own magazines and books, bypassing the Authorized Literary Channels, and initiating a revolution in poetry. More "established" presses grew out of that revolution—New Directions, Grove Press, City Lights—and a whole new poetry arose outside the purview and control of the "Reviews" located in the radical work of Walt Whitman, William Carlos Williams, Gertrude Stein, H.D., and other outlier poets. 1955 saw the publication of Paul Blackburn, Gregory Corso, Robert Creeley, Lawrence Ferlinghetti and others who arose out of that resistance. It was also the year of the historic Gallery Six reading in San Francisco, the ensuing legal brouhaha over censorship of Ginsberg's "Howl," and the surging fame of the Beats. It was the build up to the wild creative energy that erupted in the 60s and early 70s.

For me, a naïve 20ish poem writer stumbling into this world, Olson's essay was earthshaking. I know that's a cliché, but being from California and having been through some serious earthquakes, I can't think of a better way to describe the sudden liquification of everything solid. It challenged the static categories and hierarchies of the world I grew up in and announced a new sense of order specifically located in *stance*, a way of being *in* the world and *toward* the world, physically, mentally, and spiritually, body, mind, and soul—unified, indistinguishable, embraced in a way of holding yourself. And specifically holding yourself in relation to and within *relational process.* That stance addressed poetry as a mode of knowledge tied to the arrangement of its sounding, where sounding resonates in both its senses as a mode of measure through the emission of sound. At a time of cosmological turbulence in which the dominant social/political order—static, idealized, oppressive—was increasingly challenged by new modes of creation erupting in political, artistic, and scholarly life, Olson's sense of stance validated and enabled an active engagement with what Whitehead called *novelty.* It resonated throughout the multiplicity of *being-in-the-world,* not just in writing but every relation. As Henry Corbin put it in *The Voyage and the Messenger*, " … your mode of understanding reveals your mode of being, and … the significance revealed in your manner of understanding is *dependent* on your mode of being." Here *mode of being* manifests as *stance* which is always *in-relation-to*. It was a breach of the oppressive, white, complacent authority that ruled the roost in post-war USAmerica. Olson's sense of stance offered a way you could see through it toward some further order emerging in time.

"Projective Verse" in that sense, before it is poetics, is, on a deeper level, a source/center of resistance, an energetic linguistic reordering event. In 1953 Olson published a short essay called "The Resistance." He dedicated it to his friend, former French resistance fighter and Buchenwald survivor, Jean Riboud. In it Olson explained his sense that the world, and the human, had been finally freed from any lingering illusion of transcendental value or spiritual ennobling. Invoking the death camps of the Holocaust where "man is reduced to so much fat for soap, superphosphate for soil, fillings and shoes for sale," he argued for absolute attention to the body, to somatic being, what he later calls *proprioception.* "This is eternity. This now. This foreshortened span." The foreshortened span is not the negation of eternity. It is its realization in our world. There is no distinction between spiritual and physical because *physical* is a facet, not a limit, in Olson's thinking. Once attention is reoriented from some fantasy of a beyond that bestows value on earthly, physical existence, *physical* opens into new depths. It's a thought that Olson develops into his idea of what he came to call *a secular that loses nothing of the divine.*

Olson's sense of resistance was not instrumental. Resistance is not a prelude or path to something else—overthrowing state power or even stopping a war—though those events no doubt would have been welcome. It's about how you stand in the world, your stance. Resistance is its own end, its own "reward" rendered in a new world. Reorientation resituates you, adds perspective and depth to your vision that expands your experience and knowledge, enlarges and retunes your soul to distinguish and receive whole ranges of knowledge previously unrecognizable. "Its power," Olson writes in "The Resistance," "is bone muscle nerve blood brain a man, its fragile mortal force its old eternity, resistance." Resistance is a stance that determines how you are because that matters if you value truth. Beyond that there are no guarantees.

That same resistance is the heart of "Projective Verse." Olson's proposal about open field poetics, as significant as it is, is a projection of that resistance. And the "body," *this old eternity,* is the source of the knowledge that manifests that resistance in an unprecedented sounding of an emergent world. As in "The Resistance," "body" is not other than the physical body though it is more than modern medicine's body, more than biology's body, a container of organs and discrete systems. More, too, than the currently trendy "socially constructed body," bearer of gendered identity imposed from without which becomes within. Olson's body has neither inner nor outer. Conceived as a single folded and unfolded surface, it resonates with ancient knowledge. "This organism," as he proposes in "Projective Verse," "now our citadel never was cathedral, draughty tenement of soul, was what it is: ground, stone, wall, cannon, tower." This sense of body as foundation and source of resistance informs Olson's famous proposition on syllable and line:

> "the HEAD, by way of the EAR, to the SYLLABLE /
> the HEART, by way of the BREATH, to the LINE."

This proposal is meant neither to proscribe nor to mandate any particular writing practice. The last thing Olson wanted was a bunch of people following rules and writing like he did. Rather, it is a call to listen closely to the rhythms of your ancient, physical being, to rely on deep cellular, somatic intelligence in organizing the poem's sounding, a sounding that is a measure even as it is measured, a sounding that carries the sense of resistance that fuels the spiritual ordeal that informs the poem's composition. Resistance, in Olson's sense, is a commitment to honor the integrity of the world beyond the Given, beyond the medical body, beyond biology, beyond history as repetitive closure. It's a commitment to Merleau-Ponty's *lived body* in the emergent novelty of creation.

At the time Olson composed "Projective Verse," he had recently left both his job at the Office of War Information and Roosevelt's Democratic Party, disillusioned by the corporatization of politics. His one publication at the OWI was an appeal to Spanish-speaking Americans to renew American democracy and fight fascism. Soon after, the Roosevelt administration replaced him and his boss at the OWI, the poet

Archibald McLeish, with a Coca-Cola executive. He witnessed USAmerica's increasing duplicity as it inflicted reactionary violence around the world, often to overthrow democratically elected governments in the name of "democracy," and tolerated (in some cases, supported) racist Jim Crow violence in its backyard, while proclaiming itself as "the home of the free." He saw how the rhetoric of "America-the-beautiful" was a mask behind which predatory capitalism devoured and destroyed the earth for profit. The resistance of "Projective Verse" in that context was a mode of address in writing grounded in unflagging attention to the real as it emerged, attention to the energies of creation both cosmological and personal, which are identical. *As above, so below* as Hermetic philosophy has it. Although with Olson, *above* and *below* cease to exist and become one thing that consists of both—*body*.

At 75 years old "Projective Verse" continues to reverberate with resistance, with essential information we require to deal with the process we find ourselves inevitably entangled in. It's not about answers or rules. Olson never meant it as more than a provocation. "[T]hese notes," he wrote, "… are meant, I hope it is obvious, merely to get things started." It is an *opening* and *opening* never ages the way a commodity does in relation to a market. We continue to start and start again, that eternal instauration, even as the essay continues to open, not toward some further exclusion or prescription that becomes an identity, but toward an always further *wholeness* through the inclusion of the excluded: "… having considered how each of us must save himself in his own fashion, and how much, for that matter, each of us owes to the non-projective, and will continue to owe, as both go along side each other." There are no do's and don't's in the manner of Pound's lists. There is a provocation to pay attention to your *somatic self*, resist already determined form/knowledge, and incorporate what's excluded. In other words, to open.

In 1968, in the face of a world being torn apart over USAmerica's duplicitous imperial ambitions and self-congratulatory delusions, and a national poetry that failed to recognize and resist the imposition of that so-called "reality," "Projective Verse" spoke to me of the necessity to pay attention to the incomplete, the flawed, the broken, the corrupt, the excluded. It pointed beyond aesthetics to the possibility of poetry rooted in resistance and transformation. It offered a mode of integrity, a language—syllable, word, sentence, syntax—which exemplified how to attend and respond to the world's dynamic monstrousness, to this mysterious process we find ourselves in. Resistance is not instrumental, a means to an end. It is the end as the end is nothing other than how we are to be here now.

Introduction

MIRIAM NICHOLS

> When a body "encounters" another body, or an idea another idea, it happens that the two relations sometimes combine to form a more powerful whole, and sometimes one decomposes the other, destroying the cohesion of its parts. And this is what is prodigious in the body and the mind alike, these sets of living parts that enter into composition with and decompose one another according to complex laws. The order of causes is therefore an order of composition and decomposition of relations, which infinitely affects all of nature. (Deleuze on Spinoza 19)

I am writing this introduction to "Projective Verse" in 2025, 75 years after Olson fired off a first draft of his now-famous essay on poetics. Things have changed. In 1950, the spectacle of the new military technologies of World War II was fresh and scary; now the nuclear threat has become wallpaper back of global crises ranging from serious environmental damage to an endless succession of U.S.-backed regional wars. In 1944, Olson left a position in the Office of War Information and a possible career with the Democratic Party because he felt he could not act freely (Clark 84-85); now the globalization of finance and the international tangle of supply chains have compromised the agency of political actors of any stripe. In the early *Maximus Poems*, written around the time of "Projective Verse," Olson complained about the ill-effects of television and advertising on independence of mind (*MP* I.13, p. 17; *MP* I.71, p. 75); now the digital revolution has invaded all public and private spaces, including human attention spans. Olson took Alfred North Whitehead and Carl Jung as companions in thought and mentors in philosophy and psychology; we are on the far side of feminist theory, postmodernism, deconstruction, identity politics, and decolonizing discourses, all of which have been mobilized by readers against Olson over these 75 years for the sins of a poetic practice that has struck them as too epic, too male-centered, and too white.[1] So with "Projective Verse" so firmly in the rear view mirror, if indeed it is visible at all to contemporary readers of poetry, the question would seem to be why republish this essay now?

I would like to propose that for all the world-things that we don't share with Olson, there is a problematic that we do share and it is significant enough to warrant a careful re-reading of Olson's response to it in "Projective Verse" and in the projective practice of the *Maximus Poems*. By *problematic* I mean a widely shared world condition of multiple dimensions—social, cultural, economic, and political. I will try to describe this thing with a detour through Hannah Arendt's *Between Past and Future*. To the best of my knowledge, Arendt is *not* a source for Olson; I cite her because the coincidence of her assessment of the post-war Euro-American situation with that of Olson speaks to my point about the broad effects of a dilemma that both of them understood and faced differently at mid-20th century. Arendt's analysis of the impact on a culture of losing its religious and ancestral bannisters resonates with Olson's perception of a civilizational wipeout. Arendt proposes that religion, tradition, and authority are entwined dimensions of thought and experience that once secured a bridge between past and future. With the failure of this bridge—signposted by Kierkegaard, Marx, and Nietzsche in her analysis—public life is without the means to cohere.[2] Of course the dating of the deconstruction of western civilization varies mightily: does it start with Galileo's decentering of the earth? With Cartesian doubt? With the 17th century enlightenment and the consequent long, slow divergence between science and the humanities, fact and value? With Nietzsche's announcement of the death of God? With the 20th century world wars? With the Frankfurt School and post-war French theory?

For many writers, artists, theorists, and political activists in the latter half of the 20th century, the great collapse was cause to rejoice; after all, civilizations based on a Greco-Roman / Judeo-Christian heritage had uplifted the white male paradigm at the expense of everyone else. Yet

Arendt speaks of the "ominous silence that still answers us whenever we dare to ask, not 'What are we fighting *against*' but 'What are we fighting *for*?'" (27). She proposes that "the very key words of political language—such as freedom and justice, authority and reason, responsibility and virtue, power and glory—[have evaporated] leaving behind empty shells with which to settle almost all accounts, regardless of their underlying phenomenal reality" (15). The dismantling of a civilization does not resolve the problem of what to replace it with or how to live with social differences we don't like. So Olson writes in "Letter 10" of the *Maximus Poems*, "And how, now, to found, with the sacred & profane—both of them—wore out" (*MP* I.45, p. 49).

To draw attention to the ongoing difficulty of founding, I turn to Canadian journalist, Carol Off. In her new book, *At a Loss for Words* (2024), Off argues that the words we use for public life have worn out: "Words that we rely on to define and defend our civil society," she says, "are either put to work for a different ideological agenda or gutted of their meanings, the values they once stood for mocked and distorted. We are rapidly losing key language. As with nature, if we no longer have the words, we no longer have what they stand for" (1-2). Examples? Off devotes a chapter each to freedom, democracy, truth, woke, choice, and taxes. More than fifty years ago, Arendt was chasing comparable terms back to their Greco-Roman origins in an effort to refresh their meanings. So, for instance, she proposes that the Roman understanding of authority was linked to authorship (*Between Past and Future* 122); power was supposed to stay with the people; authority with the senate, so that "where force is used, authority itself has failed" (93). Olson, responding to the same hollowing out of value terms, would go behind these classical roots—the "western box" he called them—to the archaic, on a similar mission.[3]

Arendt called it pearl diving,[4] the ransacking of history for elements of current use. In the absence of an agreed-upon real, some thinkers and artists looked to past civilizational models to inspire or unsettle the present. Pound's retelling of Odysseus's descent to the underworld in "Canto I" holds the story. Repositioned in the 20th century, the tale suggests a metaphor for world alienation. To the Odyssean question of how to get home from here, the ghosts crowd around, competing for the living blood they need in order to speak. Olson's "handsome sailor" is a recurrent Odyssean figure in the *Maximus Poems*, variously expressed in Ishmael, the Gloucester fishers, Billy Budd, Christ, and Osiris. The poems themselves are the voyage. A descent to the underworld of myth and history, however, does not resolve the cultural battles in which we are still immersed. In a post-foundational era, the Odyssean question becomes existential ("I set out now / in a box upon the sea" (*MP* II.203, p. 373)), meaning that there is no available *historical* response to the quest for home.[5] What we hold in common is simply our presence on earth, not this or that history. And so we are stuck with the problem that Arendt outlines so clearly: "to live in a political realm with neither authority nor the concomitant awareness that the source of authority transcends power and those who are in power, means to be confronted anew, without the religious trust of a sacred beginning and without the protection of traditional and therefore self-evident standards of behavior, by the elementary problems of human living-together" (141). If anything, these "elementary problems" are now more intense than they were for Olson's generation.

So how, then, does "Projective Verse" abide with the difficulties in a way that gives Olson's essays and poems lasting currency? I see two major moves. First, is Olson's focus on the body and its embeddedness in the physicality of the world. "Projective Verse" famously begins with three dicta on "composition by field":

> 1) a poem is energy transferred from where the poet got it … all the way over to, the reader
> 2) FORM IS NEVER MORE THAN AN EXTENSION OF CONTENT
> 3) ONE PERCEPTION MUST IMMEDIATELY AND DIRECTLY LEAD TO A FURTHER PERCEPTION (CPr 240)

These points speak to a constant circulation of stimuli between human physiology and its perceived externalities—no dualism here between the mind and body. Poets receive data from their surrounds and activities, inflect that data through their perceptual intelligence, and project it outward to the reader. The form of the poem will come out of the on-going eventfulness of this circular activity. As reenactment of an event ("one perception must ... lead to a further perception") rather than commentary about an event, the poem leaves open higher level value terms. Instead, it situates the poet among the thought-things of the poem, as a participant in a form-making process rather than master of the field. Olson found Alfred North Whitehead's philosophy of organism companionable to the projective because Whitehead proposes a cosmos in which things are mutually constitutive. Organisms shape themselves through the prehensive process—the reception or rejection of data—they do not precede it. The body is key because as it takes form, it becomes the locus of memory and experience which are the means of a unique inflection of genetic material and hence of creative agency. In his copy of *Process and Reality,* Olson wrote in the margin, "The end of the subject-object thing—Wow!"[6]

In 1950, Olson had not yet begun his careful re-readings of Whitehead and Jung, but he had the idea that the poet needed to "[get] rid of the lyrical interference of the individual as ego" (*CPr* 247). Through this decentering, the poet might "achieve an humilitas sufficient to make him of use" (*CPr* 247). *Humilitas* is built into the logic of Olson's method and stance through embodiment: it is the capacity to remain in one's own skin and to participate from that situatedness in the larger world of species life and historical artefact (*CPr* 247). If the poet reaches for epic scale, it is still the poet speaking, not a disembodied voice that claims all timespaces, or commandeers words such as freedom and democracy, truth and justice. Such a strategy is a route less-travelled to the decentering of western humanism than that of the deconstructive philosophies or negative dialectics: the deconstructive focus on the indeterminacy of language *suspends* the saying of act and value; the situated voice *historicizes* its sayings. The justification of the projective "dogma," Olson says, is its "useableness" (*CPr* 240), not its truth or falsehood or stranglehold on the real. Otherwise said, a situated voice cannot command belief; it has to show rather than tell.

It follows from Olson's projective perspective that each person is tasked with seeing the world for him or herself. This is simply unavoidable in an era without external foundations. In "Letter 2," for example, Olson writes, "… tell you? ha! who / can tell another how / to manage the swimming?" (*MP* I.5, p. 9). The early *Maximus Poems* are full of *eyes*—"in all heads, / to be looked out of," Olson says (*MP* I.29, p. 33). Such an expectation—that everyone see the world freshly for themselves—is scarcely credible. Yet Olson writes, "So few need to, / to make the many / share (to have it, / too)" (*MP* I.29, p. 33). The poet's job—the job of any artist—is to bring forward new articulations and alignments of things, new things to be seen—or as Olson says in "Projective Verse II,"[7] "The poem's job is to be able to attend, and to get attention to, the variety of order in creation" (15). This view of cosmic becoming emphasizes matter in motion, constantly making and remaking itself as organisms—and ideas too—combine, break down, and re-form into new relationships.

This brings me to my second point: induction is a way of beginning again when value terms have worn out. Through the saying of who did what when, Olson moves behind and toward such terms without ever possessing them. Certainly *attention* and *care* are important words in the early *Maximus Poems*, but we have to reach for these words through an abundance of anecdotes. The sea captain John Smith, writing in 1626, had an eye "for what New England offered, / what we are other than theocratic" (*MP* I.50, p. 54). The Gloucester fishers, Olson and Burke, show skill at a dangerous trade and sharpness of attention (*MP* I. 27, p. 31). Stevens, the ship builder, displays care and creativity in his craft—"was the first [in New England] to make things, / not just live off nature" (*MP* I.31, p. 35). Or when a man such as Olson's landlord, Stephen Papa, is ashamed to ask for the rent, one gets a glimpse of empathy and decency (*MP* I.90, p. 94). Radical induction moves back behind the husks of value words that have worn out through use and abuse, not to claim these terms again for the poet (the *occupation* of such words would constitute an abuse of authority) but to show through story and image how judgement might be cultivated.

Right here, I think, might be the place to remember Olson's hostility to sociology, "this dreadful beast, some average and statistic" (*CPr* 297). Social signifiers—class, race, sex, gender, or ethnicity—perpetually move between foreground and background in social significance depending on the political context. When political pressure eases off, they shatter into the uniquenesses of those they name. In a projective practice, response to circumstance and event, rather than social category confers identity. "[F]elicity / resulting from a life of activity in accordance with'" (*MP* I.38, p. 42), Olson writes, and then "in accordance with what?" Instead of answering the question, he offers a definition of buoyancy and the story of a Gloucester storm (*MP* I.38-39, pp. 42-43). One has to find out what one is in accordance with by responding to chance and circumstance. The reference to buoyancy suggests that one is always "swimming" in the human universe—one is always somewhere and in motion. There is no getting out of that.

On a planet now staggering from the weight of us, I think there is an argument to be made for big picture thinking like that of Olson. Achille Mbembe, for example, talks about the "in-common" and what that might look like (*Brutalism* 2020; English translation 2024). In his last book of interviews, Bruno Latour asks what it might mean to really *land* on earth (*How to Inhabit the Earth*, 2022; English translation 2024). The environment is not something we are inside, Latour says, but something that we continually make in interaction with other entities. Both Latour and Isabelle Stengers in her *Making Sense in Common* (2020; English translation 2023) draw inspiration from Whitehead for philosophies that challenge the bifurcation of nature into active subjects and passive objects. Latour suggests that we need to start the civilizational endeavor again by re-describing our habitudes. Old political configurations of right and left may give place to alliances based on maps of habitability (48)—what we live on and what we live *off* ("what you depend on defines who you are" (41)). The role of the arts is to help us imagine new forms of agency. "For Whitehead," Stengers writes, "the possibility of an original response to what is socially given is what makes the difference between living and non-living societies" (126).

With all the ill will in the world, the human species still displays a plurality of social modes and life forms, although the effects of continuing conflict, genocide, and indifference to the earth may yet get us to wipeout. We live at a time when physical bodies are intensely subjected to will and idea through distancing technologies such as digital culture, big pharma, commercial-state surveillance, and military technologies. So very much of Olson's big picture show—from the Gloucester histories, the myths and indigenous stories, the archaic traces, and the meditations drawn from Iranian and Chinese mysticism—is about performing the various ways that human groups have interacted with each other and with other beings to create modes of life on earth. "There it is, brothers," Olson says, "sitting there, for USE" (*CPr* 240).

There is no order that does not imply repression: whatever the imagination can assemble it can also deconstruct. Hence for many contemporary intellectuals and poets, critique of what exists seems to be the only irreproachable position. But no one lives in negation. We live on a variously inhabited and badly damaged planet by means of the orders we have created; when we cannot agree or no longer believe in these orders, we drift toward anarchy, violence, or authoritarianism. In this context, Olson's challenge on how to initiate a visionary republic remains urgent and consequential. Mbembe has written eloquently of what it means to live with the effects of technological creep and predatory capital (16-17) with little agency beyond the thin defense of tribalism. Technolatry and little stories, he says (13, 43). Yet here we all are, and, as Olson said, "What weeds / as explanation / leaves out, is / that chaos / is not our condition" (*MP* I.96, p. 100).

I began by talking about the hollowing out of value words. In his essays and poems, Olson offers a record of his push to construct knowing back to image (*MP* III.126, p. 503) and through image to make manifest acts and relations from which value might be arrived at inductively. Early on in his life as poet (1946), Olson had written to Ruth Benedict, a colleague at the OWI (Office of War Information), to say that "if you burn the facts long and hard enough in yourself as crucible you'll come to the few facts that matter. And then fact can be fable again" (*Selected Letters* 58). This is the plot of "Projective Verse," the practice as well as the essay. The historical anecdotes and mythical tales of Olson's writings say who did what when and in what circumstance, so to display for whoever wishes to see what kind of a one this person was or that one, what they did in their time and place, and what mattered to them. And if, through repeated telling and recognition of sameness in difference, some of these "facts" pass into exemplarity, they may become fable. Arendt, in her comments on reflective judgement, writes that value terms like courage or goodness come out of stories (*LOK* 84-85). "Most concepts in the historical and political sciences are of this restricted nature," she says; "they have their origin in some particular historical incident, and we then proceed to make it 'exemplary'—to see in the particular what is valid for more than one case" (*LOK* 85). So projective verse: to search out stories that may be "valid for more than one case," thus to consider the question of how to live together here on earth.

Notes

[1] A few examples: For a feminist reading of Olson, see Susan Howe, "Since a Dialogue We Are" and Rachel Blau DuPlessis, chapters 5 and 6 in *Purple Passages* (117-168); for a poststructuralist discussion of Olson, see Andrew Ross, *The Failure of Modernism* (95-128); for a parodic take on Olson's "Projective Verse" coming out of Language poetry see Charles Bernstein's "Introjective Verse" in *My Way* (110-112); and for commentary on Olson as a voice of American imperialism, see Heriberto Yépez, *The Empire of Neomemory.*

Michael Boughn (*Measure's Measures*) offers a rebuttal to some of these critical commentaries. David Herd's *Writing Against Expulsion* places Olson alongside Hannah Arendt and Giorgio Agamben—poetry alongside political philosophy—in a take on Olson's significance to contemporary thought about human rights.

[2] See the chapter titled "Tradition and the Modern Age" in Arendt's *Between Past and Future* (17-40). Arendt says that Kierkegaard, Marx, and Nietzsche

> challenged the basic assumptions of traditional religion, traditional political thought, and traditional metaphysics by consciously inverting the traditional hierarchy of concepts. However, neither the twentieth-century aftermath nor the nineteenth-century rebellion against tradition actually caused the break in our history. This sprang from a chaos of mass-perplexities on the political scene and of mass-opinions in the spiritual sphere which the totalitarian movements, through terror and ideology, crystallized into a new form of government and domination. (26)

Arendt explicates her view that totalitarianism was a new political form of the 20th century in her *Origins of Totalitarianism.*

[3] In his article "'Deep Time,'" Archaeology and the Post-Romantic Paradigm," André Spears discusses the importance of archaic civilizations as inspiration for moderns wrestling with the disasters of the first and second World Wars.

[4] Here is Arendt in her Introduction to Walter Benjamin's *Illuminations.* This section of her essay is called "The Pearl Diver":

> Insofar as the past has been transmitted as tradition, it possesses authority; insofar as authority presents itself historically, it becomes tradition. Walter Benjamin knew that the break in tradition and the loss of authority which occurred in his lifetime were irreparable, and he concluded that he had to discover new ways of dealing with the past. In this he became a master when he

> discovered that the transmissibility of the past had been replaced by its citability and that in place of its authority there had arisen a strange power to settle down, piecemeal, in the present to deprive it of "peace of mind," the mindless peace of complacency. (38)

[5] My comments are about Euro-American cultures. "Home" requires a more nuanced discussion in the context of Indigenous cultures that have been interrupted and damaged by settler colonialism and that are now actively re-building bridges to their ancestral heritage and traditional territories.

[6] Robin Blaser records this comment in "The Violets," his essay on Olson's marginalia in Whitehead's *Process and Reality.* Here is the relevant passage. Blaser is quoting Whitehead:

> This is the problem of the solidarity of the universe [Olson writes in the margin, "Wow!"]. The classical doctrines of universals and particulars, of subject and predicate, of individual substances not present in other individual substances, of the externality of relations, alike render this problem incapable of solution. The answer given by the organic philosophy is the doctrine of prehensions, involved in concrescent integrations, and terminating in a definite, complex unity of feeling. To be actual must mean that all actual things are alike objects. (Blaser 218; Whitehead II.I.VI, p. 56)

The underlinings are Olson's. This passage refers to Whitehead's account of the formation of organisms through positive or negative prehension. Prehension is Whitehead's word for the process by which atom-like minims of nature—"actual entities" he calls them—attract or repulse each other to form the societies that we recognize as living things. Blaser records the following:

> From the underlined word *objects*, Olson draws a line to the bottom of the page and writes: "The end of the subject-object thing—Wow." ("Violets" 218)

[7] *The Principle of Measure in Composition by Field: Projective Verse II* is a posthumous publication drawn from the Charles Olson Research Collection at the Thomas J. Dodd Research Center, University of Connecticut Libraries.

It was edited by Joshua Hoeynck and published as a chapbook by Chax Press in 2010. The archival original consists of seven typed manuscript pages plus a footnote acknowledging Whitehead. In his introduction, Hoeynck notes that Olson's was working from the chapter titled "Strains" in *Process and Reality* (10).

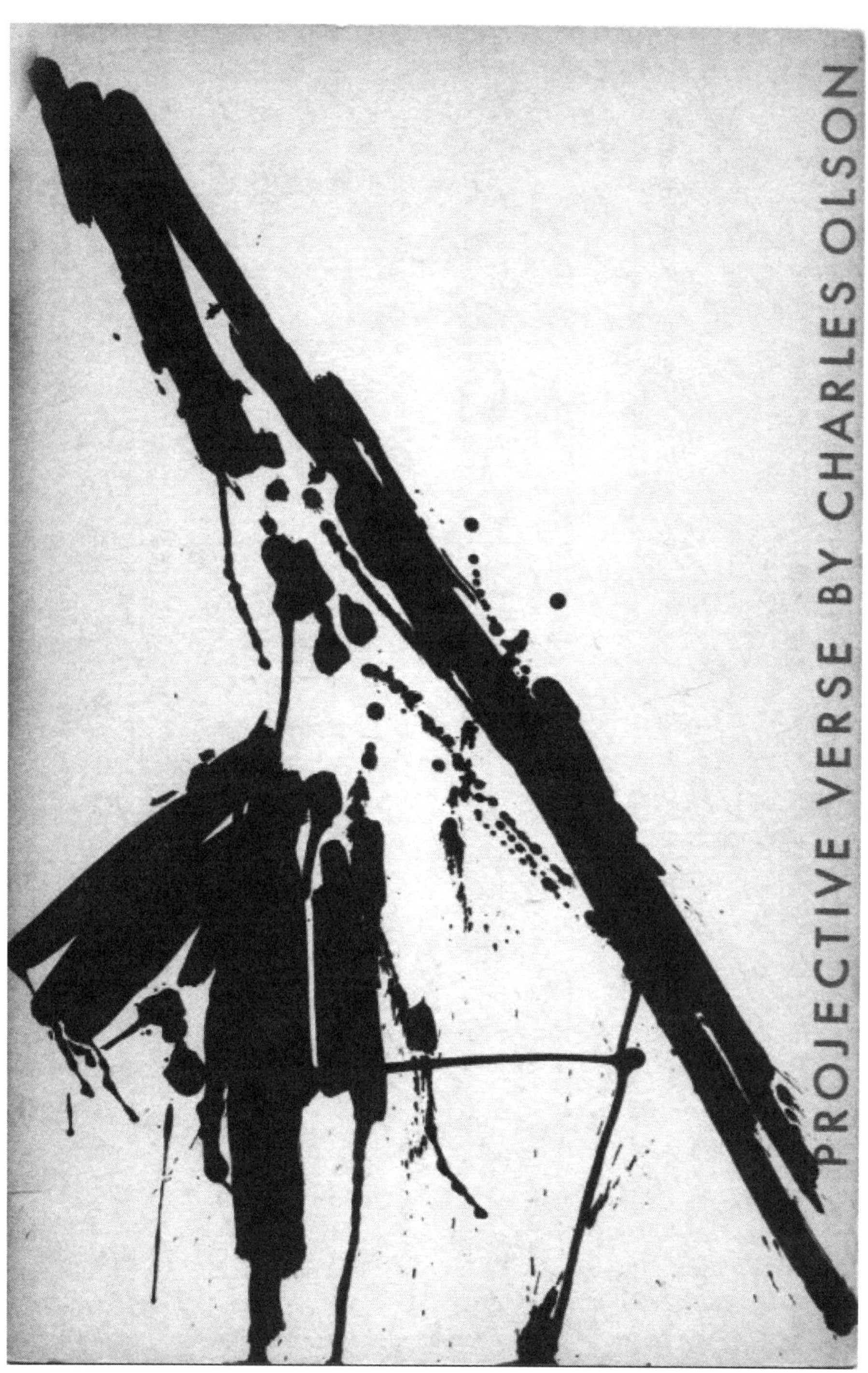
PROJECTIVE VERSE BY CHARLES OLSON

PROJE
CTIVE
VERSE
CHARES
OLSON

PROJECTIVE VERSE

(projectile (percussive (prospective

vs.

The NON-projective

CHARLES OLSON

(or what a French critic calls "closed" verse, that verse which print bred and which is pretty much what we have had, in English & American, and have still got, despite the work of Pound & Williams:

it led Keats, already a hundred years ago, to see it (Wordsworth's, Milton's) in the light of "the Egotistical Sublime"; and it persists, at this latter day, as what you might call the private-soul-at-any-public-wall)

Verse now, 1950, if it is to go ahead, if it is to be of essential use, must, I take it, catch up and put into itself certain laws and possibilities of the breath, of the breathing of the man who writes as well as of his listenings. (The revolution of the ear, 1910, the trochee's heave, asks it of the younger poets.)

I want to do two things: first, try to show what projective or OPEN verse is, what it involves, in its act of composition, how, in distinction from the non-projective, it is accomplished; and II, suggest a few ideas about what that stance does, both to the poet and to his reader. (The stance involves, for example, a change beyond, and larger than, the technical, and may, the way things look, lead to new poetics and to new concepts from which some sort of drama, say, or of epic, perhaps, may emerge.)

I

First, some simplicities that a man learns, if he works in OPEN, or what can also be called COMPOSITION BY FIELD, as opposed to inherited line, stanza, over-all form, what is the "old" base of the non-projective.

(1) the *kinetics* of the thing. A poem is energy transferred from where the poet got it (he will have some several causations), by way of the poem itself to, all the way over to, the reader. Okay. Then the poem

itself must, at all points, be a high energy-construct and, at all points, an energy-discharge. So: how is the poet to accomplish same energy, how is he, what is the process by which a poet gets in, at all points energy at least the equivalent of the energy which propelled him in the first place, yet an energy which is peculiar to verse alone and which will be, obviously, also different from the energy which the reader, because he is a third term, will take away?

This is the problem which any poet who departs from closed form is specially confronted by. And it involves a whole series of new recognitions. From the moment he ventures into FIELD COMPOSITION— puts himself in the open— he can go by no track other than the one the poem under hand declares, for itself. Thus he has to behave, and be, instant by instant, aware of some several forces just now beginning to be examined. (It is much more, for example, this push, than simply such a one as Pound put, so wisely, to get us started: "the musical phrase," go by it, boys, rather than by, the metronome.)

(2) is the principle, the law which presides conspicuously over the composition, and, when obeyed, is the reason why a projective poem can come into being. It is this: FORM IS NEVER MORE THAN AN EXTENSION OF CONTENT. (Or so it got phrased by one, R. Creeley, and it makes absolute sense to me, with this possible corollary, that right form, in any given poem, is the only and exclusively possible extension of content under hand.) There it is, brothers, sitting there, for USE.

Now (3) the *process* of the thing, how the principle can be made so to shape the energies that the form is accomplished. And I think it can be boiled down to one statement (first pounded into my head by Edward Dahlberg): ONE PERCEPTION MUST IMMEDIATELY AND DIRECTLY LEAD TO A FURTHER PERCEPTION. It means exactly what it says, is a matter of, at all points (even, I should say, of our management of daily reality as of the daily work) get on with it, keep moving, keep in, speed, the nerves, their speed, the perceptions, theirs, the acts, the split second acts, the whole business, keep it moving as fast as you can, citizen. And if you also set up as a poet, USE USE USE the process at all points, in any given poem always, always one perception must must must MOVE, INSTANTER, ON ANOTHER!

So there we are, fast, there's the dogma. And its excuse, its usableness, in practice. Which gets us, it ought to get us, inside the machinery, now, 1950, of how projective verse is made.

If I hammer, if I recall in, and keep calling in, the breath, the breathing as distinguished from the hearing, it is for cause, it is to insist upon a part that breath plays in verse which has not (due, I think, to the smothering of the power of the line by too set a concept of foot) has not been sufficiently observed or practiced, but which has to be if verse is to advance to its proper force and place in the day, now, ahead. I take it that PROJECTIVE VERSE teaches, is, this lesson, that that verse will only do in which a poet manages to register both the acquisitions of his ear *and* the pressures of his breath.

Let's start from the smallest particle of all, the syllable. It is the king and pin of versification, what rules and holds together the lines, the larger forms, of a poem. I would suggest that verse here and in England dropped this secret from the late Elizabethans to Ezra Pound, lost it, in the sweetness of meter and rime, in a honey-head. (The syllable is one way to distinguish the original success of blank verse, and its falling off, with Milton.)

It is by their syllables that words juxtapose in beauty, by these particles of sound as clearly as by the sense of the words which they compose. In any given instance, because there is a choice of words, the choice, if a man is in there, will be, spontaneously, the obedience of his ear to the syllables. The fineness, and the practice, lie here, at the minimum and source of speech.

> O western wynd, when wilt thou blow
> And the small rain down shall rain
> O Christ that my love were in my arms
> And I in my bed again

It would do no harm, as an act of correction to both prose and verse as now written, if both rime and meter, and, in the quantity words, both sense and sound, were less in the forefront of the mind than the syllable, if the syllable, that fine creature, were more allowed to lead the harmony on. With this warning, to those who would try: to step back here to this place of the elements and minims of language, is to engage speech where it is least careless— and least logical. Listening for the syllables must be so constant and so scrupulous, the exaction must be so complete, that the assurance of the ear is purchased at the highest— 40 hours a day— price. For from the root out, from all over the place, the syllable comes, the figures of, the dance:

> "Is" comes from the Aryan root, *as*, to breathe.
> The English "not" equals the Sanskrit *na*, which
> may come from the root *na*, to be lost, to perish.
> "Be" is from *bhu*, to grow.

I say the syllable, king, and that it is spontaneous, this way: the ear, the ear which has collected, which has listened, the ear, which is so close to the mind that it is the mind's, that it has the mind's speed....

it is close, another way: the mind is brother to the sister and is, because it is so close, is the drying force, the incest, the sharpener...

it is from the union of the mind and the ear that the syllable is born.

But the syllable is only the first child of the incest of verse (always, that Egyptian thing, it produces twins!). The other child is the LINE. And together, these two, the syllable *and* the line, they make a poem, they make that thing, the—what shall we call it, the Boss of all, the "Single Intelligence." And the line comes (I swear it) from the breath, from the breathing of the man who writes, at the moment that he writes, and thus is, it is here that, the daily work, the WORK, gets in, for only he, the man who writes, can declare, at every moment, the line its metric and its ending— where its breathing, shall come to, termination.

The trouble with most work, to my taking, since the breaking away from traditional lines and stanzas, and from such wholes as, say, Chaucer's *Troilus* or S's *Lear*, is: contemporary workers go lazy RIGHT HERE WHERE THE LINE IS BORN.

Let me put it baldly. The two halves are:

the HEAD, by way of the EAR, to the SYLLABLE
the HEART, by way of the BREATH, to the LINE

And the joker? that it is in the 1st half of the proposition that, in composing, one lets-it-rip; and that it is in the 2nd half, surprise, it is the LINE that's the baby that gets, as the poem is getting made, the attention, the control, that it is right here, in the line, that the shaping takes place, each moment of the going.

I am dogmatic, that the head shows in the syllable. The dance of the intellect is there, among them, prose or verse. Consider the best minds you know in this here business: where does the head show, is it not, precise, here, in the swift currents of the syllable? can't you tell a brain when you see what it does, just there? It is true, what the master says he picked up from Confusion: all the thots men are capable of can be entered on the back of a postage stamp. So, is it not the PLAY of a mind we are after, is not that that shows whether a mind is there at all?

The elements of language are finite, but the poet through his attentiveness (PLAY of mind) is the person who makes use of words in a particular sophisticated way.

And the threshing floor for the dance? Is it anything but the LINE? And when the line has, is, a deadness, is it not a heart which has gone lazy, is it not, suddenly, slow things, similes, say, adjectives, or such, that we are bored by?

For there is a whole flock of rhetorical devices which have now to be brought under a new bead, now that we sight with the line. Simile is only one bird who comes down, too easily. The descriptive functions generally have to be watched, every second, in projective verse, because of their easiness, and thus their drain on the energy which composition by field allows into a poem. *Any* slackness takes off attention, that crucial thing, from the job in hand, from the *push* of the line under hand at the moment, under the reader's eye, in his moment. Observation of any kind is, like argument in prose, properly previous to the act of the poem, and, if allowed in, must be so juxtaposed, apposed, set in, that it does not, for an instant, sap the going energy of the content toward its form.

It comes to this, this whole aspect of the newer problems. (We now enter, actually, the large area of the whole poem, into the FIELD, if you like, where all the syllables and all the lines must be managed in their relations to each other.) It is a matter, finally, of OBJECTS, what they are, what they are inside a poem, how they got there, and, once there, how they are to be used. This is something I want to get to in another way in Part II, but, for the moment, let me indicate this, that every element in an open poem (the syllable, the line, as well as the image, the sound, the sense) must be taken up as participants in the kinetic of the poem just as solidly as we are accustomed to take what we call the objects of reality; and that these elements are to be seen as creating the tensions of a poem just as totally as do those other objects create what we know as the world.

The objects which occur at every given moment of composition (of recognition, we can call it) are, can be, must be treated exactly as they do occur therein and not by any ideas or preconceptions from outside the poem, must be handled as a series of objects in field in such a way that a series of tensions (which they also are) are made to *hold*, and to hold exactly inside the content and the context of the poem which has forced itself, through the poet and them, into being.

Because breath allows *all* the speech-force of language back in (speech is the "solid" of verse, is the secret of a poem's energy), because, now, a poem has, by speech, solidity, everything in it can now be treated as solids, objects, things; and, though insisting upon the absolute difference of the reality of the verse from that other dispersed and distributed thing, yet each of these elements of a poem can be allowed, once the poem is well composed, to keep, as those other objects do, their proper confusions.

Which brings us up, immediately, bang, against tenses, in fact against syntax, in fact against grammar generally, that is, as we have inherited it. Do not tenses, must they not also be kicked around anew, in order that time, that other governing absolute, may be kept, as must the space-tensions of a poem, immediate, contemporary to the acting-on-you of the poem? I would argue that here, too, the LAW OF THE LINE, which projective verse creates, must be hewn to, obeyed, and that the conventions which logic has forced on syntax must be broken open as quietly as must the too set feet of the old line. But an analysis of how far a new poet can stretch the very conventions on which communication by language rests, is too big for these notes, which are meant, I hope it is obvious, merely to get things started.

Let me just throw in this. It is my impression that *all* parts of speech suddenly, in composition by field, are fresh for both sound and percussive use, spring up like unknown, unnamed vegetables in the patch, when you work it, come spring. Now take Hart Crane. What strikes me in him is the singleness of the push to the nominative, his push along that one arc of freshness, the attempt to get back to word as handle. (If logos is word as thought, what is word as noun, as, pass me that, as Newman Shea used to ask, at the galley table, put a jib on the blood, will ya.) But there is a loss in Crane of what Fenollosa is so right about, in syntax, the sentence as first act of nature, as lightning, as passage of force from subject to object, quick, in this case, from Hart to me, in every case, from me to you, the VERB between two nouns. Does not Hart miss the advantages, by such an isolated push, miss the point of the whole front of syllable, line, field, and what happened to all language, and to the poem, as a result?

I return you now to London, to beginnings, to the syllable, for the pleasures of it, to intermit:

> If music be the food of love, play on,
> give me excess of it, that, surfeiting,
> the appetite may sicken, and so die.
> That strain again. It had a dying fall,
> o, it came over my ear like the sweet sound
> that breathes upon a bank of violets,
> stealing and giving odour.

What we have suffered from, is manuscript, press, the removal of verse from its producer and its reproducer, the voice, a removal by one, by two removes from its place of origin *and* its destination. For the breath has a double meaning which latin had not yet lost.

The irony is, from the machine has come one gain not yet sufficiently observed or used, but which leads directly on toward projective verse and its consequences. It is the advantage of the typewriter that, due to its rigidity and its space precisions, it can, for a poet, indicate exactly the breath, the pauses, the suspensions even of syllables, the juxtapositions even of parts of phrases, which he intends. For the first time the poet has the stave and the bar a musician has had. for the first time he can, without the convention of rime and meter, record the listening he has done to his own speech and by that one act indicate how he would want any reader, silently or otherwise, to voice his work.

It is time we picked the fruits of the experiments of Cummings, Pound, Williams, each of whom has, after his way, already used the machine as a scoring to his composing, as a script to its vocalization. It is now only a matter of the recognition of the conventions of composition by field for us to bring into being an open verse as formal as the closed, with all its traditional advantages.

If a contemporary poet leaves a space as long as the phrase before it, he means that space to be held, by the breath, an equal length of time. If he suspends a word or syllable at the end of a line (this was most Cummings' addition) he means that time to pass that it takes the eye— that hair of time suspended— to pick up the next line. If he wishes a pause so light it hardly separates the words, yet does not want a comma— which is an interruption of the meaning rather than the sounding of the line— follow him when he uses a symbol the typewriter has ready to hand:

"What does not change / is the will to change"

Observe him, when he takes advantage of the machine's multiple margins, to juxtapose:

"Sd he:
    to dream takes no effort
        to think is easy
            to act is more difficult

    but for a man to act after he has taken thought, this!
is the most difficult thing of all"

Each of these lines is a progressing of both meaning and the breathing forward, and then a backing up, without a progress or any kind of movement outside the unit of time local to the idea.

There is more to be said in order that this convention be recognized, especially in order that the revolution out of which it came may be so forwarded that work will get published to offset the reaction now afoot to return verse to inherited forms of cadence and rime. But what I want to emphasize here, by this emphasis on the typewriter as the personal and instantaneous recorder of the poet's work, is the already projective nature of verse as the sons of Pound and Williams are practicing it. Already they are composing as though verse was to have the reading its writing involved, as though not the eye but the ear was to be its measurer, as though the intervals of its composition could be so carefully put down as to be precisely the intervals of its registration. For the ear, which once had the burden of memory to quicken it (rime & regular cadence were its aids and have merely lived on in print after the oral necessities were ended) can now again, that the poet has his means, be the threshold of projective verse.

II

Which gets us to what I promised, the degree to which the projective involves a stance toward reality outside a poem as well as a new stance towards the reality of a poem itself. It is a matter of content, the content of Homer or of Euripides or of Seami as distinct from that which I might call the more "literary" masters. From the moment the projective purpose of the act of verse is recognized, the content does— it will— change. If the beginning and the end is breath, voice in its largest sense, then the material of verse shifts. It has to. It starts with the composer. The dimension of his line itself changes, not to speak of the change in his conceiving, of the matter he will turn to, of the scale in which he imagines that matter's use. I myself would pose the difference by a physical image. It is no accident that Pound and Williams both were involved variously in a movement which got called "objectivism." But that word was then used in some sort of a necessary quarrel, I take it, with "subjectivism." It is now too late to be bothered with the latter. It has excellently done itself to death, even though we are all caught in its dying. What seems to me a more valid formulation for present use is "objectism," a word to be taken to stand for the kind of relation of man to experience which a poet might state as the necessity of a line or a work to be as wood is, to be as clean as wood is as it issues from the hand of nature, to be shaped as wood can be when a man has had his hand to it. Objectivism is the getting rid of the lyrical interference of the individual as ego, of the "subject" and his soul, that peculiar presumption by which western man has interposed himself between what he is as a creature of nature (with certain instructions to carry out) and those other creations of nature which we may, with no derogation, call objects. For a man is himself an object, whatever he may take to be his advantages, the more likely to recognize himself as such the greater his advantages, particularly at that moment that he achieves an humilitas sufficient to make him of use.

It comes to this: the use of a man, by himself and thus by others, lies in how he conceives his relation to nature, that force to which he owes his somewhat small existence. If he sprawl, he shall find little to sing but himself, and shall sing, nature has such paradoxical ways, by way of artificial forms outside himself. But if he stays inside himself, if he is contained within his nature as he is participant in the larger force, he will be able to listen, and his hearing through himself will give him secrets objects share. And by an inverse law his shapes will make their own way. It is in this sense that the projective act, which is the artist's act in the larger field of objects, leads to dimensions larger than the man. For a man's problem, the moment he takes speech up in all its fullness, is to give his work his seriousness, a seriousness sufficient to cause the thing he makes to try to take its place alongside the things of nature. This is not easy. Nature works from reverence, even in her destructions (species go down with a crash). But breath is man's special qualification as animal. Sound is a dimension he has extended. Language is one of his proudest acts. And when a poet rests in these as they are in himself (in his physiology, if you like, but the life in him, for all that) then he, if he chooses to speak from these roots, works in that area where nature has given him size, projective size.

It is projective size that the play, *The Trojan Women*, possesses, for it is able to stand, is it not, as its people do, beside the Aegean—and neither Andromache or the sea suffer diminution. In a less "heroic" but equally "natural" dimension Seami causes the Fisherman and the Angel to stand clear in *Hagoromo*. And Homer, who is such an unexamined cliche that I do not think I need to press home in what scale Nausicaa's girls wash their clothes.

Such works, I should argue— and I use them simply because their equivalents are yet to be done— could not issue from men who conceived verse without the full relevance of human voice, without reference to where lines come from, in the individual who writes. Nor do I think it accident that, at this end point of the argument, I should use, for examples, two dramatists and an epic poet. For I would hazard to guess that, if projective verse is practiced long enough, is driven ahead hard enough along the course I think it dictates, verse again can carry much larger material than it has carried in our language since the Elizabethans. But it can't be jumped. We are only at its beginnings, and if I think that the *Cantos* make more "dramatic" sense than do the plays of Mr. Eliot, it is not because I think they have solved the problem, but because the methodology of the verse in them points a way by which, one day, the problem of a larger content and of larger forms may be solved. Eliot is, in fact, a proof of a present danger, of "too easy" a going on the practice of verse as it has been, rather than as it must be, practiced. There is no question, for example, that Eliot's line, from "Prufrock" on down, has speech-force, is "dramatic", is, in fact, one of the most notable lines since Dryden. I suppose it stemmed immediately to him from Browning, as did so many of Pound's early things. In any case Eliot's line has obvious relations backward to the Elizabethans, especially to the soliloquy. Yet O.M. Eliot is *not* projective. It could even be argued (and I say this carefully, as I have said all things about the non-projective, having considered how each of us must save himself after his own fashion and how much, for that matter, each of us owes to the non-projective, and will continue to owe, as both go alongside each other) but it could be argued that it is because Eliot has stayed inside the non-projective that he fails as a dramatist— that his root is the mind alone, and a scholastic mind at that (no high *intelletto* despite his apparent clarities)— and that, in his listenings he has stayed there where the ear and the mind are, has only gone from his fine ear outward rather than, as I say a projective poet will, down through the workings of his own throat to that place where breath comes from, where breath has its beginnings, where drama has to come from, where, the coincidence is, all act springs.

Letter From Charles Olson Received By E.B. Feinstein. "Prospect"

May, 1959

DEAR E. B. FEINSTEIN,

Your questions catch me athwart any new sense I might have of a 'poetics'. (The best previous throw I made on it was in *Poetry NY* some years ago – on Projective Open or Field verse versus Closed, with much on the *line* and the *syllable*.

The basic idea anyway for me is that one, that form is never any more than an extension of content – a non-literary sense, certainly. I believe in Truth! (Wahrheit) My sense is that beauty (Schonheit) better stay in the thingitself: das Ding – Ja! – macht ring (the attack, I suppose, on the 'completed thought,' or, the Idea, yes? Thus the syntax question: what is the sentence?)

The only advantage of speech rhythms (to take your 2nd question 1st) is illiteracy: the non-literary, exactly in Dante's sense of the value of the vernacular over grammar – that speech as a communicator is prior to the individual and is picked up as soon as and with ma's milk ... he said nurse's tit.) In other words; speech rhythm only as anyone of us has it, if we come on from the line of force as piped in as well as from piping we very much have done up to this moment – if we have, from, that 'common' not grammatical source. The 'source · question is damned interesting today – as Shelley saw, like Dante, that, if it comes in, that way, primary, from Ma there is then a double line of chromosomic giving. (A) the inherent speech – (thought, power) the 'species,' that is; and (B) the etymological: this is where I find 'foreign' languages so wild, especially the Indo-European line with the terrific advantage now that we have Hittite to back up to. I couldn't stress enough on this speech rhythm question the pay-off in *traction* that a non-literate, non-commercial and non-historical constant daily experience of tracking *any* word, practically, one finds oneself using, back along its line of force to Anglo-Saxon, Latin, Greek, and out to Sanskrit, or now, if someone wld do it, some 'dictionary' of roots which wld include Hittite at least.

I'll give in a minute the connection of this to form if capturable in the poem, that is, the usual 'poetics' biz, but excuse me if I hammer shortly the immense help archaeology, and some specific linguistic scholarship – actually, from my experience mainly of such completely different 'grammars' as North American Indians present, in the present syntax hangup: like Hopi. But also Trobriand space-Time premises. And a couple of North California tongues, like Yani. But it is the archaeology *behind* our own history proper, Hittite, for the above reason, but now that Canaanite is known (Ugaritic) and Sumerian, and the direct connection of the Celts to the Aryans and so to the Achaean-Trojan forbears which has *slowed* and opened the speech language thing as we got it, now, in our hands, to make it do more form than how form got set by Sappho & Homer, and hasn't changed much since.

I am talking from a new 'double axis': the replacement of the Classical representational by the *primitive-abstract* ((if this all sounds bloody German, excuse the weather, it's from the east today, and wet)). I mean of course not at all primitive in that stupid use of it as opposed to civilized. One means it now as 'primary,' as how one finds anything, pick it up as one does new-fresh/first. Thus one is equal across history forward and back, and it's all levy, as present is, but sd that way, one states … a different space-time. Content, in other words, is also shifted – at least from humanism, as we've had it since the Indo-Europeans got their fid in there (circum 1500 BC) ((Note: I'm for 'em on the muse level, and agin 'em on the content, or 'Psyche' side.

Which gets me to yr 1st question – "the use of the Image." "the Image" (wow, that you capitalize it makes *sense*: it is *all* we had (post-circum *The Two Noble Kinsmen*), as we had a sterile grammar (an insufficient 'sentence') we had analogy only: images, no matter how learned or how simple: even Burns say, allowing etc and including Frost! Comparison. Thus representation was never off the dead-spot of description. Nothing was *happening* as of the poem itself – ding and zing or something. It was referential to reality. And that a p. poor crawling actuarial 'real' – good enough to keep banks and insurance companies, plus mediocre governments etc. But not Poetry's *Truth* like my friends from the American Underground cry and spit in the face of 'Time.'

The Image also has to be taken by a double: that is, if you bisect a parabola you get an enantiomorph (The Hopi say what goes on over there isn't happening here therefore it isn't the same: pure 'localism' of space-time, but such localism can now be called: what you find out for yrself (*'istorin*) keeps all accompanying circumstance.

The basic trio wld seem to be: topos/typos/tropos, 3 in 1. The 'blow' hits here, and me, 'bent' as born and of sd one's own decisions

for better or worse (allowing clearly, by Jesus Christ, that you do love or go down)
if this sounds 'mystical' I plead so. Wahrheit: I find the contemporary substitution of society for the cosmos captive and deathly.

Image, therefore, is vector. It carries the trinity via the double to the single form which one makes oneself able, if so, to issue from the 'content' (multiplicity: originally, and repetitively, chaos – Tiamat: wot the Hindo-Europeans knocked out by giving the Old Man (Juice himself) all the lightning.

The Double, then (the 'home' /heartland/of the post-Mesopotamians AND the post-Hindo Eees:

At the moment it comes out $\frac{\text{the Muse ('world'}}{\text{the Psyche (the 'life'}}$

You wld know already I'm buggy on say the Proper Noun, so much so I wld take it Pun is Rime, all from tope/type/trope, that built in is the connection, in each of us, to Cosmos, and if one taps, via psyche, plus a 'true' adherence of Muse, one does reveal 'Form'

in other words the 'right' (wahr-) proper noun, however apparently idiosyncratic, if 'tested' by one's own experience (out plus in) ought to yield along this phylo-line (as the speech thing, above) because – *decently* what one oneself can know, as well as what the word *means* – ontogenetic.

The other part is certainly 'landscape' – the other part of the double of Image to 'noun'. By Landscape I mean what 'narrative'; scene; event; climax; crisis; hero; development; posture; all that *meant* – all the substantive of what we call literary. To animate the scene today: wow: You say "orientate me." Yessir. Place it!

again

I drag it back: Place (topos, plus one's own bent plus what one *can* know, makes it possible to name.

O.K. I'm running out of appetite. Let this swirl – a bit like Crab Nebula – do for now. And please come back on me if you are interested.
Yrs.

CHARLES OLSON

A Note On the Last Twenty Years of Olson Studies

AMMIEL ALCALAY

The focus of our project is to celebrate and consider "Projective Verse" at age 75. At the same time, "Projective Verse" can't be separated from Olson's other work. Given the retrospective nature of our endeavor, and the tendency for many close to Olson over the long haul to adhere to terms of reference and perspective rooted in earlier contexts, we thought it would be useful to offer a brief survey of what has actually amounted to a remarkably live and active period in more recent Olson studies and activities.

Taking 2005 as a somewhat arbitrary starting point, given that the first *OlsonNow* event took place at the St. Marks Poetry Project, this note is meant to survey some aspects of the Olson landscape over the past 20 years, pointing to activities, scholarship, translation, and the emergence of new archival materials and correspondence.

Organized by the late Fred Dewey, Michael Kelleher, and myself, *OlsonNow* was intended to demonstrate what a "conference on poetics" might look like if it was organized as an extended town meeting. Without adding a trademark to the idea, others took it on and created their own iterations and the concept served to at least provide an address of sorts around which various affinities could find common reference while preparing the ground for further thought, publication, and activity.

Such further activities included the Olson Centenary held at Clark University in 2010, along with events celebrating Olson in Gloucester, MA, which saw the beginnings of what would become the annual Olson Lecture at the Cape Ann Museum, as both Diane di Prima and Michael Rumaker appeared. Another Centenary Conference was held at Simon Fraser University, an important node of Olson studies and affinities, spearheaded, of course, by Ralph Maud.

In many ways, this interim period between 2005 and 2010 provided the impetus for what would become *Lost & Found: The CUNY Poetics Document Initiative*, and my own very Olson centered book, *a little history* (2013). An attempt was made at *Lost & Found* to reacquaint readers with the Buffalo Olson Memorial Lectures, instituted by Robert Creeley, events that seemed like some lost Dead Sea scrolls of US poetics. "Olson Memorial Lectures" by Robert Duncan, Diane di Prima, and Ed Dorn came out, along with the selected correspondence between John Wieners and Olson.

Presently, Onur Ayaz is working on the correspondence between Olson and Jonathan Williams for *Lost & Found*, focusing on the publication period of the first set of *Maximus* poems. In a recent series, Khaled al-Hilli's edition of *Sargon Boulus: "This Great River"—Translating the Beats into Arabic*, partially explores the Iraqi poet Sargon Boulus's interpretation of "Projective Verse" and the influence it had on the contemporary and avant-garde poetic scene from the late 1960s in Arabic, a virtually unknown site of Olson influence. Interestingly enough, this reach may even have come to inform contemporary Iraqi scholar Aseel Abdul-Lateef Taha's paper on Olson's "The Kingfishers," with its insistence on the poem as a key early example of anti-colonial and anti-imperialist poetics and thought.

Meanwhile, in the background, various plans to house the Maud/Olson Library were in the works, from the transportation of it from Vancouver to Gloucester, to its housing at the Gloucester Writers Center, its installation just a bit further down the road on East Main, until finding a true place of respite at the Cape Ann Museum Library and Archives in 2021 where it can now be perused and consulted.

The year 2011 saw the first volume of *Los Poemas de Maximus*, translated into Spanish by Ricardo Cázares, followed in 2015 by his translation of *Poemas de Maximus IV, V, VI*, both published in Mexico, a labor of love whose resonance is still in play. Sandwiched in-between this extraordinary continental "homecoming," an English translation of Heriberto Yépez's 2007 text *El Imperio de la Neomemoria* appeared in 2013 as *The Empire of Neomemory.* Faced with various rejoinders from Jack Hirschman, Amiri Baraka, Kenneth Warren, myself, and many others, the most articulate reinstatement of Olson's continental importance, as expressed by the time he spent in Mexico, didn't come until Dennis Tedlock's 2017 volume mentioned below and Edgar Garcia's wide-ranging and ground-breaking *Signs of the Americas: A Poetics of Pictography, Hieroglyphs, and Khipu* (2020).

In direct relation to "Projective Verse," two of the most significant pieces of scholarship to note are Joshua Hoeynck's archival text *The Principle of Measure in Composition by Field: Projective Verse II* (2010), and Dennis Tedlock's *The Olson Codex: Projective Verse and the Problem of Mayan Glyphs* (2017). Though not explicitly directed at "Projective Verse," two other recent works of great significance are David Herd's *Writing Against Expulsion in the Post-War World: Making Space for the Human*, and the forthcoming and very long awaited revised and expanded edition of *The Special View of History*, edited by the late Ralph Maud and John Faulise, with an introduction by Gary Grieve-Carlson and an afterword by Joshua Hoeynck (2026).

In *Writing Against Expulsion*, Herd makes the bold and brilliant move of putting Olson the poet and thinker into colloquy with Hannah Arendt and Frantz Fanon, as decisive figures through whom we can think about the world we presently inhabit. The revised edition of *The Special View* includes new archival material, expanding significantly on the original Oyez Press edition prepared by Ann Charters. In addition, the bookends by Joshua Hoeynck and Gary Grieve-Carlson, scholars of a different generation than many traditional "Olsonites," promise to be of great interest. Both David Herd and Joshua Hoeynck have edited volumes of scholarly articles that provide excellent overviews of the state of Olson studies, Herd's *Contemporary Olson* (2015), and Hoeynck's *Staying Open: Charles Olson's Sources and Influences* (2019), both featuring a wide array of subjects and scholars of different generations and orientations.

And the letters keep coming: the Gloucester centered *Charles Olson: Letters Home-1949-1969*, edited by David Rich (2010); *After*

Completion: The Later Letters of Charles Olson and Frances Boldereff, edited by Sharon Thesen (2012); *Evidence of What Is Said: The Correspondence between Ann Charters and Charles Olson about History and Herman Melville*, edited by Ann Charters, (2015); Benjamin Hollander's unique call for letters addressed to Olson posthumously, *Letters to Olson* (2016); *An Open Map: The Correspondence of Robert Duncan and Charles Olson*, edited by Robert J. Bertholf and Dale M. Smith (2017); and *Collected Letters of Charles Olson and J.H. Prynne*, edited by Ryan Dobran (2017). Also notable is a full edition of Robert Duncan's lectures on Olson, *Imagining Persons: Robert Duncan's Lectures on Charles Olson*, edited by Robert J. Bertholf and Dale M. Smith (2017).

Present *Lost & Founders* at the almost completion of dissertation stage, Sam O'Hana Grainger and Onur Ayaz, continue to do astonishing work: a recent article by O'Hana Grainger in the *Chicago Review* examines Olson's work at the Office of War Information, while Ayaz's work on pedagogy—both through his own practice and a close study of Olson's teaching career—brings forth exciting new possibilities for modeling a generative Olson who can light a fire under students who may never have read a poem. Finally, we would truly be remiss to not mention *A Life of Olson: & A Sequence of Glyphs on Points of his Life, Work and Times*, by Ed Sanders (2020), and the very recent *T.S. Eliot and Charles Olson—Young Tom and Charlie: Two American Poets at Home in Gloucester*, edited and introduced by Ann Charters, with commentaries by Amanda Cook and Samuel Charters (2024).

Afterword

CHARLES STEIN

Projective Verse and Its Stance Toward Reality[1]

1

Seventy-five years of "Projective Verse" has witnessed, as Miriam Nichols' Introduction suggests, several generations of reactions to the poetry roughly composed under the ideas behind its "stance." Olson states at the beginning of his essay that he will be taking "a stance towards reality" that is appropriate to possibilities newly available for the composition of poetry. I have often thought that there is in place today, across the entire human world, what I call a *default ontology*: a picture of Being itself, not necessarily held by anyone, but towards which much of today's serious thinking tends; namely, that the only thing that really exists is "information": technical bits, bytes, and pixels, of which external "objective" things consist, and by which all "internal" subjective states can be described. Charles Olson, in his "Projective Verse" essay, and in the *Maximus Poems* composed under its "stance towards reality," strenuously opposed this "information only" ontology—decades in advance of our current "digital age." Olson wants us to take our bodily senses as the primary way we have for knowing reality. All that today's and much of the future's "artificial intelligence" makes possible—its ever-more capable and ever-more inclusive capacity for simulation—is based on the reduction of all phenomena to their information content. Direct perception loses its directness. We are implicitly asked to distrust our experience and correct it, not with further examination of what is there before us, but with quantified "data" in the form of information. Both our physical presence in the cosmos and the world's presence to ourselves, are reduced to the manner in which they can be represented digitally. Resistance to this default view can be cultivated by taking a stance that rejects it. However, as Michael Boughn insists in the Preface to this book, to take a stance *at all* in a manipulated simulation of a world is *already* resistance.

Olson studied and used in particular the writings of C.G. Jung, Alfred North Whitehead, Henry Corbin and Albert Einstein to establish for himself a "concretistic methodology": his insistence that the materials used in his poem be chosen on the basis of their concrete presentation to the poet, either in sensory perception or through coming upon thought and story in texts or other forms of documentary presentation.

2

A *stance*: a bodily attitude, as if *facing up to* the character of whatever is coming towards one or simply welcoming what is just now coming on the scene in a definite manner. A stance does not *describe* a perspective on what is, it actually *takes* one. Taking it, you are physically right there, together with the concrete things that are happening. If you cannot or do not take a stance intentionally your life is lived through the attitudes of others. Unreflected notions coming from the media, the people you are in association with, the "society" quite broadly, dictate and order how you act, what you do, how you make preferences and choices in and for your world. Still, Olson is not necessarily proposing to the poets (or anyone else) that they should adopt *his* stance, though he certainly does take one in his essay; but more importantly, that each poet and each living person should discover and actively take up their own. Olson's *The Special View of History* speaks of history itself as what each of us finds out for him or herself, regarding what is happening or what others say about it. History itself is an aggregate of stances. And those stances are taken up by each one of us on our own terms.

"Projective Verse" asks each one of us to stand before reality as she or he comes to find or indeed imagine it. "Reality is unfinished business," (Olson, *Special View*, 27) he will say (and I want to say—it still is!). If the poets are, as Olson opines, "the only pedagogues left," this might be so only to the extent that they take reality itself on their shoulders. The poet provides our picture of the world. Olson positions what he calls an *imago mundi*, an image of the world, as a fundamental feature of human nature. The *imago mundi* is the "unfinished business" that the innate power to find and project form must address. The earth and what happens on it belong to any one of us insofar as we take it to be ours and complete it by giving it form—in poetry, in story, in dreams, or in how we understand our living acts. The seriousness of poetry derives from how it embodies such a stance and projects it onto and into the actual world in which it occurs.

3

Though conventional literary theory concerns writings that are already "literature" in the canonical sense, "Projective Verse" removes the poem from literature altogether and opens an inquiry as to what the concrete situations for making poetry actually are. For Olson the poem is a material utterance and claims our attention for the same reasons that the physical things of nature also do—because they are there in our presence and show qualities that engage our interest. Poems are produced by and from the poet's body—feeling from *breath*, and mind through the play of *syllables*—in whatever dialectical varieties the poet's actual speech is couched. They share their being as utterances with the palaver of fisherman, with the peculiarities of Seventeenth Century American prose, with Walt Whitman's democratic "blab of the pave." They are not first of all objects in a literary tradition, constrained by the "elevated" tone of canonized poetry. They will find their own kind of "elevation" within, not above, the concrete conditions of utterance. The point importantly is not that the poem is a literal *transcription* of what is more authentically spoken out-loud; rather, the way in which the poet's body projects its rhythms and determines its own music should not be ignored in the act of writing and the act of reading.

4

Since the decades immediately following World War II, our cultural and intellectual contexts have changed many times over. America and its allies had beaten the Nazis, but a new opposition to the Soviet Union was endangering the peace. Olson had rejected the anti-Soviet policies of the Truman administration and abandoned what had looked like a promising political career in the Democratic Party to work out a stance to the world more to his own sense of things. It would not be a stance assimilable to the oncoming world of postwar global politics. It did not see Communism as a possible answer to human suffering, but neither did it see it as an inevitable foe. Olson did see much of Capitalist motivation and practice as making that which he affirmed invisible or impossible. "In the present go/ nor right nor left;/ nor stay /in the middle," he writes early in *The Maximus Poems* (Olson, *Maximus,* I.54/58). It would be a stance that late-twentieth century politics could not interpret and often misconstrued. Olson explicitly takes a stance that, understood politically, is set apart from these positions. He asks for acts that are particular to concrete situations, not dictated by party politics. It is not easy therefore to estimate his "position" in the common political spectrum, and attempting to do so gets in the way of hearing the specificity involved in so much of his dealing with history.

5

Soon after Olson's death in 1970, important French texts by Jacques Derrida, Jacques Lacan, Michel Foucault (as well as important German texts of Martin Heidegger)[2] appeared in translation. We were soon treated to Jean Baudrillard's perception that contemporary America (and the rest of the world in close pursuit) was heading toward a frank valorization of *simulation*—imitation, representation, "information"—as the primary factors in what is. Baudrillard imagines our world as a theme park with imitations of other theme parks as *its* basic theme—Disneylands or Disney Worlds each with its fake "Las Vegas" for one's hazardless holiday enjoyment (no gambling in Disney World!). The only reality beyond these simulacra would be something like the parking lot. You either live in a simulation or a humdrum reality with no style, no energy, and no meaning beyond immediate utility. Derrida's "deconstruction of the metaphysic of Presence" demanded a problematization of immediate experience that for many of us reiterated Baudrillard's grim picture.[3]

6

Of course Olson had no knowledge of any of this as it was brewing in France during the last years of his life and never present in English during that time. And yet it is plausible to me that Olson was proposing, and indeed performing, an act of resistance to a picture of the world—an ontology—that he already sensed was coming on. In "Projective Verse" he proclaims a way of being in one's body and on earth—what a later poem in the *Maximus* series proposes as an "actual earth of value." Maximus rejects the prospect of a simulated world in principle and on as many levels as he was able to give concrete attention to.

For Olson the body itself lives on earth as a *knowing* animal. Its sensory apparatus, when properly tuned to what is present and what is happening in, through, by, and around it is not merely and fundamentally conditioned by what its culturally determined mental apparatus puts in front of it. Being situated in the body—its organs and its capacity for direct awareness—should serve as a defense against what was in a few generations to be discernible as a "Digital Age."

7

In recent years, information technology has placed the rapidly accelerating powers of simulation palpably in our faces. Our world today offers ever-more-accurate *fake* versions of aspect after aspect of human experience, from robot domestics, factory workers, and on-line sex partners to the production of academically acceptable prose compositions and the broadcast content of the daily news ("fake news"). Is resistance to this covering of everything with an information patina any longer possible? Can private experience and perceptive attention hold out against what Peter Lamborn Wilson called "the surveillance state"—the easy policing of every aspect of our existence and the availability of all the information that describes us for individually targeted political propaganda and the endless mendacity of "personalized" advertising? Whether effectively opposable or not, today there are young people (and very old ones) for whom a world replaced by its information is intolerable.

Of course there were only giant mainframe computers in the late 1940s and 1950s, but the basic intellectual work for developing computational technology had been accomplished. Alan Turing had shown in effect that digital coding could represent anything at all that came to appearance. The objective world could be read as information, but then so could subjective experience. Norbert Weiner had begun a long process of attempting to harmonize human beings with the new form of technological invention (Weiner, *Cybernetics, Human Use).* Olson knew Weiner's work and was already wary of the new way of thinking which at one point he dubbed "the statistical" and condemned, as the Olympian deities condemned the Titans, to "Tartaros," a dank and morally neutral habitation of dead gods (Olson, *Maximus*, II.163/333)! In "Maximus from Dogtown IV" Olson included a translation of a passage from Hesiod's *Theogony* actually *celebrating* the Titans whom a patriarchal Zeus had conquered and thrown into Tartaros, but in this poem, he sees the very being of the oncoming world as reduced to its statistics, that is, its information—and characterized by the dismal qualities of that sad place.

8

Cognitivity—the capacity to know—affects every act of perception. "Projective Verse" takes a stance toward a knowing of reality that places perception front and center, both in the practice of verse and in everyday life. Like an ontology, a stance entails a sense of what is; but unlike an ontology, it does not offer itself to be challenged and progressively corrected or indeed "deconstructed." The work of knowing and understanding—all argumentation for instance—precedes taking the stance that enacts it. A stance puts an implicit understanding into action and tests it, not by argument, but by paying attention and responding to what attention finds. The practice of "Projective Verse" puts thinking back into the cosmic context about which, and amidst which, it occurs.

Though taking a stance is something other than adopting a philosophical position, the intellectual underpinnings for it may help one understand something of the cognitive framework for Olson's stance, and the reasons he had for taking it. Olson took aspects of the thinking of C.G. Jung, Alfred North Whitehead, Henry Corbin, and the implications of Einstein's theories of Relativity as of particular importance for his own work, and judged that they should be important to others.

9

In a series of notes to himself, in planning for *Maximus IV, V, VI,* the volume of *Maximus* that succeeded the first *Maximus Poems*, he proposes that he must adopt a psychology based on Jung (see Stein, *Chrysanthemum*), but made less nebulous by the metaphysics of mathematician and philosopher Whitehead. The latter had collaborated with Bertrand Russell on *The Principles of Mathematics* and authored a full-blown metaphysical system (mainly in *Process and Reality*), perhaps the last to be attempted in Western philosophy. In the later *Maximus Poems,* Olson does use the thought of Jung and Whitehead to frame the work conceptually, and he did find other deeply connected conceptual material in Henry Corbin, the French scholar of Islamic mysticism.

Corbin, together with Jung and Whitehead, would aid Olson in his determination to project as he would put it, "a secular that loses nothing of the divine" (Boughn, *Measure's*, 12). "Projective Verse" makes assertions that show a use of Einstein's relativistic "reference frames" as necessary for establishing an objective picture of the universe. (A reference frame provides the "coordinates" that locate in space and time the phenomena under consideration, but shows the phenomena from a single, "a special" [subjective] point of view.) Without a subjective frame, the objective facts cannot be given exact meaning.

Olson borrows Jung's notion of a primordial world of forms as psychically manifest "archetypes." However, rather than placing these structures in a vaguely delimited "Collective Unconscious," he finds them in the physical body itself—as the bodily organs. Olson understood that the bodily organs exist as concretely present in the individual but as universal to the species. Their characteristics carry the essential properties of Jung's archetypes, which, though universal in structural form and psychological relevance, occur individuated in any person's psychic life. So for Olson the archetypes are the organs. The organs are the archetypes. The dynamic sources for psychically charged content are concretely materialized in the body itself. Again, the organs are both universal and particular; they are common to the species and individuated in the body of the person. Similarly the Jungian archetypes are universal to the species and manifest in particular ways in the individual's psyche. The existence in one site of the universal and the individual is the grounds for their cultural and cosmical pertinence. Olson concretizes the archetypes and will find them in the most concretely realized actual experiences (Olson, *Proprioception*, 17);[4] but, at the same time, they are the means through which the cosmos appears for any person. In coordination with this he will recognize that Whitehead's metaphysics features what is *actual* as real. Actual things and occurrences are not the mere shadows of Platonic forms or "examples" of general concepts underlying; rather, they are essentially more real than those things and occurrences. They are what he calls "actual occasions" or "actual events." Such occasions or events comprise all the things of which the universe is composed in their actual occurrence in the cosmos and not, for instance, off somewhere in a separable "universe of discourse." Abstract thought is not ignored, however, but is accounted for by what Whitehead calls "eternal objects"—atemporally abiding forms that provide actual entities with their identities. The eternal objects, like the Platonic forms, are not in time but only come to appear through their "ingression" into actual occasions in the temporally extended world. Whitehead's metaphysics for Olson complements and qualifies Jung's psychology: Olson finds atemporal archetypes in the body, and that as such they embody eternal forms ingressing in the world.

Henry Corbin was a correspondent of Jung's and frequent participant in Jung's Eranos Conferences. He found in the visions of the Islamic mystics of his concern a "middle realm" or "mesocosm" between eternal ideas and the human sensorium, comprising an "imaginal" realm through which the individual soul discovers its relationship to that which transcends it. The mesocosm gives to the human imagination (for Olson, his world of poetic form) the ontological status of the middle world's own activity. Corbin's thought evolves under the imperatives of "phenomenology": the modern philosophical disciplines that assume the primary reality of human consciousness. With Einstein's relative "frames of reference," the necessity of taking human experience as requiring its own study becomes inevitable. Edmund's Husserl's proclamation of that discipline becomes well-defined in the years following Einstein's Theory of Special Relativity (1905).

10

The issues regarding the nature of sensuous immediacy fully occupied Olson and are by no means resolved in our time, in spite of the overwhelming presence of the digital and the many derogations of Derrida's "Deconstruction." Some of these Derridean assaults still remain to be answered, and reflections upon Olson and his stance may yet prove pertinent. Meanwhile the permissions granted by "Projective Verse" for bringing form into being, and addressing how a poem's content relates to its form, remain capable of being acted upon. Their invitation to welcome concrete phenomena into the poem still provides ground for any one of us to resist the ontological principle on which AI is based: that information and only information is real. Olson's stance still opens possibilities for poetry and for direct experience that resist our submission to the "information-only" ontology. Grounding our sense of being in the sensuous immediacy of what stands before us is our best, if not our only, chance of allowing "what is" to show its sacrality.

11

In poetry the appearances of being given by the poet give form to the world. The capacity—even the necessity—to generate forms is an innate and defining human characteristic.[5] Form itself is generated through our desire to perceive it. "[One] loves form only," says Maximus in his very first letter to the people of Gloucester. But "… form only comes / into existence when / the thing is born" (*Maximus*, I.3/7). The love of form is satisfied when we apply form-giving attention to concrete phenomena. The projective poet must attend the presence and contours of concrete entities as they actually appear and link them to the way the cosmos, through its concrete appearances, projects its form.

Obedience to this *concretistic* methodology shows Olson how he can release Jung's archetypes from their vaguely symbolic existences and make them relevant to his own concerns. Olson will discover through his own body, through his powers of giving form to what he perceives, and through his own dreams and poetic visions that the archetypes are themselves concrete entities: our bodily organs, "slung" in the body's dark interior, what Olson sees in place of the analytical psychologist's notion of the unconscious (Olson, *Proprioception*, 81).

Jung and Whitehead together provide a way of thinking about cognitivity—about the nature of knowing—and how knowing has a sacred nature. Olson, paraphrasing Whitehead, will say that God is just "man, taking thought." Once again: though a stance does not *describe* a perspective on what is, it actually *takes* one. Taking thought should have the seriousness as befits its sacred character.

12

A stance is an ontology put to use. Concepts—cognitions—are in use when embodied in a stance toward reality. When that stance regards concrete existence as that towards which one *takes* one's stance, even abstractions like Whitehead's "Eternal Objects" or Henry Corbin's "mesocosm" can be understood in the actual contexts of their being applied: in Olson's context, to make a poem that delivers an *image of the world* and that puts its governing ontology to use. "Projective Verse" makes that possible, and *The Maximus Poems* brings it to appearance. Thought does not only occur in the critical discourse that comes to affirm or critique it, but in creative work where cognition in its atemporal character (as in Whitehead) interacts with the time-bound, creative event which it identifies and in which it occurs. Relativity, atemporal cognition, Jung's concretized archetypes, and Corbin's mesocosm, will yield in the composition of the poetry of "Maximus" a new valorization of the earth; and this happens by establishing the positive character of matter and the earth itself in order to open new possibilities for life on this planet.

To learn to know that the earth is sacred is a work in progress for us all. Creating in the early *Maximus Poems* a picture of the nation in its concrete history as having wasted its founding possibilities, Olson devotes himself, in traditional Platonic (or revolutionary American) fashion, to producing a (probably unactionable) model for a reborn polity. He directs himself "to write a Republic / in gloom on Watch-House point" (*Maximus*, III.9/377). And to this he will append : "an actual earth of value / to construct one (Olson, *Muthologos*, 50).

13

The materials for such a construction are to be governed by the complexly executed principle that I call Olson's "methodological concretism": the new image of the nation and its earth must be dealt with in the most concrete sense available. All materials for the poem must stem from Whitehead's "actual occasions"; imagery must flow from sensuous particulars; language will be attended sensuously, material objects treated as embedded in a nexus of spatiotemporal events. Observations, documents, and experiences in general are the traces of actual occurrences and are actual occurrences themselves. The expression of particular facts must be in concrete language, using and emphasizing the most physically subtle, but emphatically present, elements of speech and writing. And the writing must show—in images, narratives, and conceptual formulations—the acts and products of its evaluations. A complete illustration of this concretism deserves an entire volume of analysis. I cannot give an example that offers the whole range of these constraints, but ask the reader to take another look at *The Maximus Poems* under the considerations I offer in this Afterword. *The Maximus Poems* themselves hazard that construction.

14

What is Projected in "Projective Verse"

Sigmund Freud's psychoanalysis and C.G. Jung's analytical psychology both make use of the psychological meaning of "projection." In both the unconscious psyche projects its contents onto the persons with whom it is connected and the world with which it deals. Olson takes Jung's cue that the individual psyche's (the soul's) contents are not limited to its repressed past as projected onto other persons and the world and rendered symbolic by spontaneous psychological creativity. The soul also projects and is governed by "archetypes." These are deeply unconscious, imageless structures that are universal to the species and project themselves as universally comprehensible, mythically charged forms in dreams, art, and cultural formations. They are the Jungian psychologist's stand-in's for disembodied Platonic ideas or for culturally transmitted mythical themes.

15

Some years after "Projective Verse" appeared in *The New American Poetry,* Olson apparently rued his use of "projection." The critical attacks on his project were never clear about how Olson used the *projective* as a general figure for expressive consciousness (a view that Olson certainly did not originally reject). But applying projectivity to writing poetry smacked for some (and even to Olson himself eventually) too much of the percussive, phallic aggression that Olson seemed to affirm in the text itself. And this certainly served to reinforce the view of Olson as boosting male identity and even implying misogyny.

Olson had in fact put three terms

(projectile (percussive (prospective

printed this way under the title of his essay as given in the Poetics appendices to *The New American Poetry*, so he was not originally innocent of the "percussive" sense of projection. In spite of this, however, for me "projection," in addition to involving a "projectile," has always suggested a geometrical sense. Projective Geometry provides structural models for things like shadows and cinema. It analyzes the way shapes of objects can be projected by a luminous source onto a "plane of projection," say a movie screen; but also how the projected forms can be transformed in the process. Change the angle of incidence between the light source and the projective surface and the shadow of the object changes shape accordingly. The object projected is a relation between it and its projector. It is not only a series of properties belonging to an object whose predicates severally define it. The aptness of that structural model has nothing to do with phallic thrust or sexual rhythmicity, or with the privileged image of humanity as essentially male. Rather, projection suggests the concrete manner in which any object *maps* itself in the way it comes to be seen. Projection induces the mapping of a given form onto another surface. For "Projective Verse" our native ability to project form is the projector. The world and its people: the screen. That ability is not inherently male, though the history of the West has suppressed its female manifestations. As a project for future humanity, this can and must be corrected.

Indeed the sense of projectivity as mapping certainly does not limit itself to the idea of projecting the image of Maximus as "patriarch," even though Maximus does present himself as a train of male heroic figures (not all of them patriarchs however). Maximus is attempting to make discriminations within the male image, not project it as male. Think of "Maximus from Dogtown" where the young Gloucester bull-fighter, Merry, is killed by his bull. Maximus shows Merry as "braggart man" whose involvement with his macho self-image destroys him. Or again, John Winthrop, first governor of Massachusetts, is called a "wanax"—a "war king" from Homeric Greek—to suggest the level of dignity he might have been afforded for his offering of the New Colony as "a city on a hill." The New World would beacon new values. It should be free of Europe's age-old corruptions and honored for rejecting the nascent capitalism of the Massachusetts Bay Company and its corporatization of fishing. Olson honors the fishermen of Cape Ann for their human ingenuity and practical skill in the struggle for existence within and up against the apparent aggression of nature: stormy seas and difficult conditions: the honest human practice of fishing versus its organization into a corporately controlled "industry." Or again, at the level of image, Maximus is androgynous: "Maximus is a whelping mother, giving birth/ with the crunch of his own pelvis" (*Maximus*, II.87/257), or "in stately motion to sing in high bitch voice the fables/of wood and stone and man and woman loved" (*Maximus*, II.10/180).

The resistance to Olson's idea of projection on aesthetic rather than on anti-patriarchal grounds may also have had to do with the revival of Expressionism in Abstract Expressionism or Action Painting which, in practice if not yet in name, had already taken place when he first drafted the piece. It was to explode at Black Mountain College under Olson's rectorship. Franz Kline, Robert Motherwell, and Robert Rauschenberg were just three exponents of it that practiced and/or taught there. What characterizes these painters was the primacy accorded their materials—paint, brush, canvas—but equally the acts of the painter's body by which the painting was expressed. Olson's attitude parallels the painters' in Black Mountain during his tenure as rector. He too is concerned with the concrete materials of his poetic work and how attention to their operations within expressive speech are never apart from contents of the poetry. In any case Olson's "projection" goes beyond the psychological and even the Expressionist senses that made "Projective Verse" something like a catch-word for free verse expressing personal affect. Olson's "expressionism," as does Abstract Expressionist painting, draws energy from a transpersonal—archetypal—source. For though the Action Painters usually did not offer a content beyond the act of painting and its gesture-like expressive character, poetic creation (but consciousness in general) involves a double or circular projection: from the world onto the poet's awareness; from morphogenic creativity onto the world. Both the world and the person of the poet give the poem content. What one loves in art is primarily form, as Olson avers early in *Maximus*, but he qualifies this in "Projective Verse" by quoting Robert Creeley's remark that "Form is never more than an extension of content." Content matters and is presented concretely and explicitly. For the painters the content is sometimes derived from the external world but it is present implicitly, not by the transfer, say, of figurative *information*.

16

"Projective Verse" has familiarly been misread as valorizing oral poetry and the performance occasion at the expense of the written text. But this misses the dichotomy that Olson actually articulates. The text itself is the reception of language as spoken and, as such, may serve as a score for further oral performance. But Olson doesn't contrast live performance to written text; rather, he calls attention to a distinction within textuality itself. There is, in the projective texts he favors, language that holds the energy proper to living speech. The projective text uses that energy to give the poetry the form inherent to that energy's motion. More traditionally written poetic texts use poetically "elevated" speech whose language is obedient to formal rules—stanza forms, meters, rhyme schemes—all of which are formulated independently of the energetic conditions under which a given poem, or even a genre of poetry, comes into being. Non-projective poetry tends to affirm and enforce the ontological assumptions of the literary culture in which it is formed, assumptions that connect externally prescribed forms to the sense of the poetry.

The projective text has its context in the concrete circumstances that demand its production. It itself is a transitional site between what the cosmos "projects" towards the poet, and a further projection that the poet sends in turn, into and onto the world.

The glory of it is that the very *reception* by the poets of the outer world's "projection" already involves acts of mind that bring to form what the world sends towards them. The outer world's projection is itself a kind of "utterance." It carries something like an intelligent *act* whose agent is simply the concrete local situation that radiates its properties, but which, when received consciously and conscientiously by the body and sentient intelligence of the poets, that intelligence functions in those properties coming to form.

Now, is the source of the act of intelligent projection person or world? For Olson it was perhaps Whitehead's God—what Olson recognizes as "the act of man taking thought." But for his readers, ready or not ready to accept that recognition, the poetry, as indeed the act of "a man taking thought," should provide materials for further creative inquiry into this question. In any case the reader becomes the theater for the originating event's further enactments. For Maximus, through his concretistic methodology and the poem's secular content, "God," in the form of a person's "taking thought," performs the sacred.

17

Subject and Object

"Projective Verse" entails a view of how perception contacts its object, as if to resolve the philosophical problem of subject-object dualism (which by the way, Deconstruction on the one hand, and digital epistemology on the other, may seem to have resolved); except that here both terms "cancel out" since the relation between them is circular. "Subject and object are given by the same evidence," as one phenomenologist put it.[6] An object and its appearance—its form—circulate *intransitively*. "Transitivity" (as opposed to "transiency" or what is "transitory") is a logical term for sequences like causality where that which comes earlier in an order cannot also appear later. Cause precedes effect. *Intransitivity* then is a violation of such an order. The forms of the world are projected onto the world, but at the same time are projected from it.

Concrete perception gives itself an object that, together with its immediate appearance, one feels must exist even when not being perceived.

But in the projective stance the object itself projects its perceivable properties, qualities, energies into (onto) the sensorium of the perceiving person; and this spontaneously and instantaneously moves the person to create a "form" of that input and project it back out onto the world. This series of phenomena is, as I say, "intransitive." The output is its own input. The object as "really there"; and with it, together with the perceptible form provided by the subject, constitute the object in its coming to appearance as both its very self and, as a made thing, a "poetic" object.

If one stops short in the circuit at the reified object, thinking its "reality" depends upon its very independence *from* the circuit, the living connection between perceiver, object, and the concrete context of their circulation simply does not appear. But perception is a living connection to its object: both are concretely and actually happening as "moments" in one circuit, bound to the temporal moments of their occurrence.

18

Imago Mundi / Mappemunde

In poetry the connection between subject and object is given as the very evidence of its own fact. An image of the world that arrives through one's own nature is clearly both. In the act of writing a poem, it comes into existence through the composition one is working to bring into being. In *Causal Mythology,* the *imago mundi* exists innately in the psyche, not as a fully-formed image, but as a potential and a demand, a form-giving activity, and the internal pressure to realize it. Maximus proclaims that he is "making a *mappemunde*" a world-map that is to "include his being" (*Maximus*, II.87/257). But clearly the image of the world at one's birth is not yet fully realized before one has first formed an image of external existence; but an internal demand or "instruction" to make such an image is born with one as something to be realized during one's life. And of course, such an image includes one's own being. One might well have already been trying to grasp one's situation prenatally. In any case, once realized, an image of the world brings with it a sense that it had been there all along. The image of the world that one in fact invents and/or discovers comes tinged with an aura to the effect that its truth has never not been the case. The potentiality for realizing an image of the world and putting or finding oneself on a map of it is there from the beginning. Like Jung's archetypes that are not yet images themselves but *potentialities* for manifesting libidinously charged images, the *imago mundi* lies waiting to be discovered through the intransitive projectivity, the form-giving aspect, of one's being. "[T]he illusory / is real enough," says Maximus (*Maximus*, 1983, II.296/126). In the course of one's existence in the world, the concrete confrontation with what exists in it does not yield a "final" metaphysical determination but an event in which the "full circuit" of object (Olson, *Collected Prose*, 162), experience, and projective occasions occur. A poem is such an occurrence; its nature as an object is inseparable from the fact that it embodies and carries further a cognitive act. But the very possibility of that cognition is, as we will see in Henry Corbin, "the Angel" of one's being; though for Olson such cognition can be ensconced in a very secular, everyday context. The quality of the ordinary does not mitigate the depth of the mystery. It explicates or complicates it. The quotidian is itself already a "mystery," and only as a "mystery in plain sight" resonates the sacred.

19

The Mesocosm and the Imaginal Realm of Henry Corbin

The great French Islamicist Henry Corbin was a correspondent of Jung's and contributor to the Jung-dominated Eranos conferences, as I mentioned above. By the 1960s he had become a familiar thinker in Jungian circles and his writing was available in English through the publication of a seminal essay in the *Eranos Yearbooks*[7] which Olson devoured, and the translation of one of his book-length studies, *Avicenna and the Visionary Recital* that Olson owned, annotated, and lifted phrases from.

In Corbin's formulation of Islamic visionary thought, the image-rich visions of the Sufis and other contemplatives mediate an imageless ultimate reality. Corbin calls this mediating realm the "mesocosm" (in Arabic *alam-al-mithal*), the "middle world." The mesocosm abides between the realm of the angels (who actively project the elements of the world and provide them with their sacred signatures) and the material world that the uninitiated senses perceive. The angel *mediates* reality by *meditating* it—but that meditation simultaneously occurs within the soul of the angel's devotee/initiate. Angelic meditation allows one to cognize the world through a specially activated power of the imagination that Corbin says produces "the imaginal." By being esoterically identified with your Angel, that is, by imagining the angel in *your* meditation imagining *you,* you *become what you really already are* and your imaginal cognition defines your imaginal world. But that cognition itself is orchestrated by your Angel, even as the Angel is itself a product of your meditation. This as we have seen was Olson's sense of the relationship between the concretely present sensuous world and human consciousness as intransitive. The Angel IS you insofar as your imaginal life finds itself open to your Angel. "Being open" to what imagination accepts as real is the only chance one has to form an authentic picture of who one is, and what the world itself can be found out to be.

The Angel does not necessarily come to appearance visually as in the familiar images of angelic beings, but its presence may occur to one under concrete, sensory situations, if apprehended through one's special capacity to imagine, that is to say, to *think* it. In this sense, one's very power to give form to the world "is" one's Angel. And the concrete apprehension of one's concrete sensory situation comes to thought through it as the mesocosm.

20

Ta'wil: "The text itself as the secret"

Corbin discovered in a library in Istanbul a series of writings by Avicenna, an Iranian thinker known in the West for his medical texts and abstruse theology. They were composed in classical Arabic, but the text

Corbin found was a Persian translation with a Persian commentary. The writings Corbin found embodied narratives replete with spiritually resonant imagery that not only delivered a soteriological message, but apparently were also intended to "initiate" the appropriately self-chosen reader into the realm of experience the texts expressed. Corbin used the French term *"récit"* (as in English "recital, tale, a telling") to characterize the Avicennan texts. *Récit* may be familiar in the special usage by Maurice Blanchot to describe his own cryptic narratives as occurring, not previous to the writing, but *in the telling itself.*[8] A *récit* then is a text whose meaning (and even whose form) is arrived at in the course of composition. The acts and events of composition constitute the writer's own visionary comportment, so their traces cannot be expunged from the final work. The reader in following the text undergoes a kind of repetition through recitation of the author's own spiritual narrative. Olson underlined "the text itself as the secret" (from page 33 in the cited edition) and inscribed it on the cover of his copy. The meaning of the text is embodied by the process rendered legible in the text itself and capable of being undergone by its reader. The reader undergoes the text's inner meaning on a journey through it. Reading *Maximus* with an understanding of the stance implied by its own production and the stance one is adopting as one reads it are quite different from sampling the text as "literature." In the one case, you are accepting *The Maximus Poems* as a *récit* in Corbin's sense, because you are really *undergoing* what it means to inhabit its meaning; in the other, you study and appreciate.

For the *récit* to draw the reader to the truth made available in its reading, the reading itself must constitute a special kind of exegesis, what the term *Ta'wil* borrowed from Avicenna entails. Ta'wil is sacred reading: "The exegesis that brings the soul back to its truth," and, he suggests, this brings the *text* back to its truth. This is possible only if it occurs as a "recitation," an initiating repetition, that brings the soul of the exegete correspondingly back to *its* truth.

Olson's primacy of the concrete allows the unimageable reality embodied concretely in a text to become intelligible to an embodied reader.

Though the angelic realm in itself is the very essence of the intelligible, that essence is not only conceptual but operates "personally" by orchestrating the cognitive music of one's concrete existence. In a sense, Corbin's mesocosm sports abstraction, but does so as if under Wallace Stevens' apt phrase, "An abstraction blooded, as a man by thought" (Stevens, *Complete Poems,* 333). It is thought itself that, inhabiting a man, renders even an abstraction a full-bodied event. For Olson that mode will prove to be the actual "human universe." Maximus quotes Corbin: "The Soul is a magnificent angel"[9]—not a magnificent *image* merely, but a living fact transforming the sensuously apparent material world into the refulgence (if not the very image) of an angelic being.

It is as if in our time, the material and the immaterial had changed places; that we tend to look to matter and the earth for what is real, and tend to look for value consistent with that understanding. Jung experienced something of this inversion, and Olson is clearly supporting that view.

In my view Jung's work in psychological theory provided terms for experiencing the sacrality of the archetypes—as it were the Platonic forms—in an age when the spirituality mediated by instituted religions no longer held the attention of the thoughtful, and the Platonic forms were commonly thought to be extinct. The sacred archetypes for Olson, however, could be recovered through secular means: a psychology that unlike Freud's was not hostile to finding apparencies of the sacred in secular manifestations.

The full inversion of heaven and earth, or the celestially imaginal and the terrestrially reified, is only suggested in Corbin, particularly in the essays included under the telling title, *Spiritual Body, Celestial Earth.* Still the sacred character of the mesocosm would apply to the actual world of the senses if the soul adopted an attitude to allow for that: for Olson the appropriate stance toward reality. The sensuous need not, indeed cannot, leave the intelligible behind; nor can the intelligible find expression without the sensible. The imaginal faculty *tinctures* experience with a sacred interiority—and is nothing other than what we in our attitudinally transported materiality will find it to be. If as Jung's work suggested to Olson the "archetypal dominant" or ideal image (Jung, *Aion*) governing the "Piscean Age" as the new "Aquarian Age"[10] comes on the scene has changed, then the new "dominant" archetypal structure no longer focuses on the celestial purity of a transcendent virgin but seeks out chthonic energy and the valor of matter. The ideal, mesocosmic image mediating the imageless transcendent might appear in material reality and concrete consciousness. Olson will find that in Corbin's studies there is an Angel that is Matter itself, and that the earth itself has an angel. For Olson the mesocosm is the world in the forms we find for it under a disciplined attention to its concrete appearances.

The Angel is imaginary; but the form by which one might rationally distinguish the Angel from reality is the product of that imagination as well. One's own imagination is the morphogenic capacity by which the material world, not only its possible angelic source, comes to apparency through, as we will see, the absolute character of Relativity.

Maximus in *The Maximus Poems* is a psycho-cosmic event whose actual character can only be grasped imaginally, but whose imagery is no longer celestial but terrestrial, historical, material, and not only *sensuously* perceptual, but *sensually*—libidinously—charged, given as the actual qualities attended to and envisioned in and of this world.

21

Alfred North Whitehead

After publishing the first volume of *The Maximus Poems* and while considering how to proceed, Olson instructed himself to adopt Alfred North Whitehead's *Process and Reality* for the cosmology of the poem and Jungian thought for its psychology (Stein, *Chrysanthemum*, 25ff). Maximus will refer directly to Whitehead in several places and speak explicitly of "eternal events" as intersecting with the concrete phenomena of experience and not excluding the dreams that announce themselves as revelatory. Maximus says:

. . . that we act somewhere

at least by seizure, that the objective (example Thucidides,[11] or
the latest finest tape-recorder, or any form of record on the spot

—live television or what—is a lie

as against what we know went on, the dream: the dream being
self-action with Whitehead's important corollary: that no event

is not penetrated, in intersection or collision with, an eternal
event (*Maximus*, II.79/249)

Olson misreads, perhaps intentionally, Whitehead's "Eternal Objects" as "eternal events." *Process and Reality* delivers a comprehensive ontology based on two sorts of existences: first, "actual entities" (also called "actual occasions") and "eternal objects." The former comprise everything that actually occurs in the world: materially complex objects, subjective experiences, and temporally extended things such as poems, philosophies, and cultures. All of the above harbor the "eternal objects" which, though not in time themselves, are potentially temporally present through their "ingression" into "concrescent" (coming together) streams of actual occasions.

The eternal objects, unlike Platonic forms, do not comprise a realm separate from the timebound, sense-delivered world; still, their atemporal, identity-bestowing character leaves open imaginative participation in mythical or speculative matters that do imply an eternal prospect. (By "eternal," by the way, Whitehead means "not in time at all"; he does not mean "forever.") Like Jung's archetypes, they are available for creative projection. Like Corbin's mesocosm, eternal objects allow essentially *unimageable* things to come to appearance in the concrete phenomena they organize and identify. Like Olson's understanding of the archetypes as the bodily organs, however, they find eternity inseparable from its concrete manifestations. That which does not in its essence exist in time, does, indeed paradoxically, *come into being*, but only through the concrete (emerging/vanishing) apprehension of what is palpably there before one. That which is essentially not in time at all comes to appearance as radically transitory but duratively extended objects, or in apparently timeless visions. Olson recognizes through Whitehead the atemporally functioning factor, not only in "sacred" visions, but in every perception through its inherent, cognitive factor. He will put Whitehead's eternal objects to use, perhaps intentionally misquoting the phrase (or accepting his own error) to emphasize even more than Whitehead, the temporal context for the occurrence in concrete experience of that atemporal character.

In the circuit between the world's projection of itself onto the poet and the poet's projection back onto the world, atemporal archetypes may function without their being held apart from the concrete circumstances in which they occur. Whitehead's eternal objects allow Corbin's angels to appear as archetypal manifestations, in special moments coloring the very world as Olson perceives it directly. Such moments are occasionally mentioned by Olson for no other reason than that noticing them *finds* them special:

> ... (some country roads
>
> have trees growing and the road
>
> turns in such a way it is special,
>
> for a few feet (*Maximus*, II.8/178)

The nervous system itself—the very organ of "noticing"—might serve as what among the bodily organs/archetypes receives the Gloucester land, sea, and sky as angelic manifestations.

22

A reader still might wonder whether, and in what sense, Olson really believed in his angels. I am reminded of the mysterious "entities" in *A Vision* that delivered to William Butler Yeats his own "metaphysical" system. (Olson, by the way, knew *A Vision* intimately (Olson, *Collected*, 141)).

Yeats famously remarks that the beings that gave him his "vision" told him that they came to bring him "metaphors for poetry." Readers immune to Yeats's occultist affiliations find in this remark a justification for skepticism about these beings, and for the notion that Yeats himself didn't "really believe" in them. But an opposite reading surely is also, if cagily, intended by Yeats, really to catch the skeptics in their obtuseness to the genuinely mysterious character of the imaginary. The poetry of Yeats that his entities inspired bears witness to the genuine mystery of poetic creation. Yeats's spirits are themselves metaphors for what allows Yeats to imagine them. Similarly, the Corbinian Angel produces the imagination that imagines it, and the sacred character of the world that contains it. This logical intransitivity is of the essence of any visionary object, and the condition of its emergence. It situates the precise role of "faith" in a secular universe: not at all "belief" in an inexplicable reality, so much as the "permission" to engage the imaginal faculty; to put the imagination to ontologically cogent, imaginal use. Olson will write of imagination itself that

> ... it sends out
>
> on the path ahead the angel
>
> it will meet (*Maximus*, II.71/241)

Though the Angel itself does not yield to explicit narrative or image, narrative and image may be shown to be transparent to the Angel's actuality in a proper exegesis, where that Angel's being is shown to be one's own. Corbin, as we saw, calls such an exegesis, *Ta'wil,* what brings the text back to its truth—possible only, as we saw, by way of "recitation" that brings the soul of the exegete back to *its* truth.

In Corbin the mesocosm, though inapprehensible to the uninitiated intellect, provides sensibly apprehensible forms for a faculty of the imagination that when activated participates in the coming to appearance of the sacred. Text and soul are treated with the same language. The exegesis by the soul of the reader brings that soul into the meanings which the text in content and process of readership bring to the same "truth."

Between the timelessly ultimate, and the apparent temporality of the cosmos, there is a mode of apparency capable of being present in image and story—present to the aspect of the imagination that *is* them by imagining them. But in oncoming time, according to Jung and Olson, that realm of image and story will be the world in the concreteness of its actual apparencies. *The Maximus Poems* presents a foretaste of, and a practice that realizes, that world.

23

Theories of Relativity

I mentioned earlier that Olson connected the role of the "reference frames" in Einstein's theories of relativity to the philosophy of Phenomenology, where human experience sits in the foreground of reality.[12] What direct perception finds is by no means a "simulation." Our sense of the cosmos as consciousness presents it to us, and what we find it to be through "taking thought" is a reality in its own right.

The perennial motive and present practice of natural science continue to seek a conceptual complex to unify the world. An intuitive complement to that scientific positivity is essential for the formation of a useful "mappemonde." Such a map must not exclude one's own being, since subjective consciousness itself is an objective fact and takes place in the cosmos, and because the subjective is formed in circulation with the object it cognizes.

In Einstein's two Theories of Relativity, presented in 1905 and 1915, the space-time continuum is "known," Olson says, but its pertinence to how we actually take in the world, or find our place in it had not yet, in 1950, completed its cultural itinerary. Our image of the cosmos must find itself in a new ontological situation. Before Relativity, phenomena at the level of concrete individual experience provided evidence for our material situation that could be conceived only through its invisible mechanistic underpinnings—the neurophysiology underlying sense-perception and the deterministic physical laws underlying that. After Relativity we can no longer base abstract theory on the confidence we enjoy in the veracity of our senses. And yet, direct perception, *pace* Derrida, like physical systems under a coordinate system and its reference frames, by being *entirely* relative, had become in a new way perfectly *definite.* What the Phenomenologists will call the "lived world" is *relatively* determined, but *determined* nevertheless. It is no longer something to be dismantled and corrected by appeal to mechanistic underpinnings described by natural science. It has its own being, its own reality, that is given directly to human experience in its own terms. Olson's "human universe" exists alongside the scientifically available one not as a merely "subjective" counterpart to it, but because subjective reality really does *happen*—its mode of appearance is as determinate as the "objective" conditions that determine it. Einstein himself thought that "relativity" misnamed what was truly an "absolute" theory: a theory about how the relative, as positively determining the appearance of things, was, thus understood, absolutely so determined. Similarly, human experience, however it is made determinate by the material, historical, and psychological conditions it is ensconced in, has its own irreducible reality, and it is that reality that brings the cosmos to an imagined form. The scientific representation of the cosmos is understood as precisely the human project that seeks to take hold of what it finds itself among.

24

Seventy-five years after its first publication, Olson's "Projective Verse" and the stance towards reality that furthers writing under its posture, remain as pertinent to our sense of reality, and suggestive of a practice within and on it, as in the first months of its publication. Olson's stance combines a "concretistic" methodology with an "intransitive" understanding of how the world connects to our image of it. Our actual presence in the present world cannot be left out of our *imago mundi,* our *mappemonde,* our sense of ourselves and the cosmos. Information can simulate everything but that presence. In an inverted sense, Deconstruction got it right. By finding the metaphysics of presence impossible to construct coherently, it *brings* to presence all that conceptual thought, taken positively, cannot represent. The world projects itself into and onto our being, and we, giving that projection form, project it back onto the world. The circuit provides the bases on which making poetry—in the sense of "Projective Verse"—can be composed and understood. It does so exactly in the way that any of us finds ourselves actually *here* in a concretely given world.

Coda

Perhaps a reader who has followed my argument will be able to see how the thinking behind Olson's stance toward reality allows one's actual experience of the cosmos to embody a sense of its sacred character. Reality in these terms cannot abide what I have been calling the information-only ontology; however, one might wish that Olson had presented more convincingly how his concretism opens onto a vision of the sacred with enough fortitude to ward off decisively that picture of the world. I don't think I want to claim that by itself Olson's stance could really have done that. Neither Olson nor anyone else can see where the ever-expanding commitment of the human project to the information exigency will take us. Will it finally erase all other human possibilities, forgetting previous ways of being human in the universe and eventually fading away through the spiritual poverty of its own enervating simulations? Or will information eventually give way before the real possibilities hidden in plain sight that information pretends to imitate but really covers over? Perhaps early on in Olson's project he thought that the path of resistance he was taking might really ward off the "Information Age"; but I don't think he died with that confidence intact. He certainly never abandoned his project and was working on his *imago mundi* through his last days in the hospital. But it was "in gloom" that he had proposed to write his "Republic," not in real hopes that he could convince even the people of his own Gloucester to adopt it. From the beginning he saw that his desire to change the very moral character of the nation was a somewhat forlorn ambition.

I would conclude with mention of my late friend Peter Lamborn Wilson and his "Temporary Autonomous Zone" (TAZ). Peter proposed that where effective resistance to an objectionable condition is not feasible, its possibility can be sustained by finding times and places where it is, if only for a brief occasion. Some years ago the "Occupy Wall Street" movement adopted "TAZ" for its own hopeful vision. "Another World Is Possible" was one of that movement's more fetching slogans. A theme in the later *Maximus Poems* that I haven't discussed here celebrated "Possibility" itself: "All men are the glories of Hera by possibility," Olson wrote. But Peter spent his last months in despair that even the temporary respite granted in spaces and times free from what he saw as universal surveillance might no longer be possible. Information is *already* surveillance. It abuses the inner life entirely by reducing it to its digital formalization. It is the final consequence of a "will to control" that has distorted human intelligence for several millennia. But neither Olson's nor Peter Lamborn Wilson's despair is a program. Another world is possible. It still is—through the marshalling of human attention in its concrete actuality, for an openness to Being that belongs to us, not in transcendence of, but directly and courageously through, what we are given to encounter.

I don't think Olson offered his stance to usher us directly into the world that his vision foresaw as possible. The sacred is suggested, certainly, through what his "taking thought" renders for him as the divine. But I think that he was after what is at stake in our thinking about poetry. Poetry itself sustains possibility. Olson presents what it is possible to entertain, so that we might try it out on our own "system." He does not enjoin each one of us to take *his* stance, but as I think I make clear at the outset, to find one's own.

Notes

[1] In these notes, page references to *The Maximus Poems* (hereafter *Maximus*) indicate both the page in the University of California Press edition and the page numbers in the original, as published by Olson, or after his death by his estate. For instance, "III.9/377" means Volume III, in the University of California Press edition, corresponding to page 9 in the original publication, and page 377 in the University of California Press version.

[2] Jacques Derrida, *Of Grammatology,* translated by Gayatri Chakravarty Spivak, Motilal Banarsidass, 1994; Jacques Lacan, Ecrits: *The First Complete English Language Edition,* translated by Bruce Fink, W.W. Norton & Company, 2007; Michel Foucault, *The Order of Things: An Archaeology of the Human Sciences,* reissue Vintage, 1994; Martin Heidegger, *Being and Time,* translated by John Macquarrie and Edward Robinson, 1962; Jean Baudrillard, *America,* reissue Verso, 2020. These dates are, except for Heidegger, their recent editions. I am mentioning them just to give a sense of some of the thinking that flourished in this country after Olson's death and what he was opposing even in advance of its appearance.

[3] I am not aware that either Derrida himself or any of his acolytes took Olson's sense of somatic and chthonic presence as an object to deconstruct. So far there has not been to my knowledge a detailed study of Olson's "stance" in comparison with the implications of Derrida's thinking, though one would be surely appropriate. But the contrast in attitude between them does bring into relief essentially different approaches to the "present" world and how one might position oneself in and towards it. Both approaches remain possibilities for our time and its future. For Derrida and his "Deconstruction," there simply is no immediate, sensually or intuitively guaranteed "picture" of the world. According to Deconstruction, unignorable ambiguities appear wherever one tries to land a sense of existence in solid, sensuously immediate terms—terms which do not rather quickly disintegrate under the Deconstructing gaze. But Olson I think does not flinch before the inevitability of this indefiniteness and proposes a stance for overcoming it in one's most

essential activity: one must take in what the world projects onto one's sensorium, and project the form one discovers for it back onto the world. Though Olson did not have Deconstructive texts or experience of its practice, he felt the pressure of an oncoming world in which immediate reality would be relentlessly replaced by simulacra: informationally-defined representations which, as is the case with Derrida's Deconstruction, erase the very concern for authentic, immediate experience.

[4] Olson speaks of the "unconscious" as the interior of the body:

> The 'cavity'/cave: probably the 'Unconscious'? That is, the interior empty place filled with 'organs'? for 'functions'?
>
> The advantage is to "place the thing, instead of it wallowing around sort of outside, in the universe, like, when the experience of it is interocaptive: it is inside us ..."

[5] In an unpublished essay titled "Economos" in the Olson archive at the University of Connecticut at Storrs, Olson speaks of two essential characteristics of human being: that we are form-making beings, which he calls "the morphic" and that we are biologically generated, which he calls "the genetic."

[6] I remember this formulation as from Jaspers, but I have been unable to locate the reference. I think it was quoted in a text by the Tibetologist, Herbert Guenther.

[7] Corbin, Henry. "Cyclic Time in Ismail Mazdaism and Ismailism," in *Man and Time, Papers from the Eranos Yearbooks 3,* edited by Joseph Campbell, Princeton University Press, 1957.

[8] *The Station Hill Blanchot Reader: Fiction & Literary Essays* (ed. George Quasha, 1999) and the essay «The Song of the Sirens,» p447, trans. Lydia Davis. "The tale [*récit*] is not the narration of an event, but that event itself, the approach to the place where that event is made to happen ...."

[9] *Maximus*, II.70/240. Here is the passage that Corbin quotes in "Cyclical Time" from the thinker about whom he is writing, one Nasir Tusi: "More active than the person himself is the thought that is thought through him, the word that is spoken by him (and personified in him). And this thought of his thought is precisely what Nasir Tusi calls the Angel of this thought (or of this word of action)." Nasir Tusi is quoted in a footnote at this point: "Every true thought, every truthful word, every good action has a spiritual … entity—that is to say, the Angel … who endows the soul, in its progressive rise, with the ability to pass easily through the successive degrees of perfection and return to its original source. Then this soul becomes a magnificent Angel *(fereshta-ye karim)*, and the angels of its thought, speech, and action become integral parts of it, setting their imprint upon it."

[10] The Precession of the Equinoxes is an astronomical phenomenon where the time of the equinoxes moves one sign "backwards" through the Zodiac approximately every 2200 years. Some astrologers understand this as giving a 2200 year cycle for "world ages," each age dominated by the equinoctial sign for that period and the zodiacal sign 180 degrees opposite that. We are presently passing from the Piscean to the Aquarian age, the opposite signs for which are Virgo, the image of heavenly "purity" for the Piscean, and Leo, a terrestrial beast for the Aquarian.

[11] Olson's spelling.

[12] The relativity of movement in space was understood as early as Descartes; namely, that the movement of a physical body in space is relative to another body in relation to which it moves, and that either body could be understood as the one in motion. But nothing like the relativity of time and space themselves was seriously countenanced before Einstein.

Epilogue

ROBERT KELLY

Often guided by recent critics who read Olson as social history, younger readers are tempted to take his body of work as societal and political commentary. No more rosebuds. Scholars often acquire a taste for *opinio* over *scientia*, taking sides instead of taking time. The time within each reader that the poem renews.

That makes me even happier today now that Station Hill Press dares bring out into sunshine the best known in one way, least understood of Olson's writings. "Projective Verse" is 75 years old, and American poetry has been shaped in so many ways by it, either directly or via the poets Olson spoke so powerfully to—Creeley, who taught us how to listen to silence; Duncan, who reminded us that intellect has feelings....

I'm saying this now because it's in "Projective Verse" that the secret shows through, the hopeless animate humanity of saying or singing: the breath. Olson dares to go to the very moment by moment operation of the human machine, our breathing, and to use that veracity, feeling, meaning, all made manifest through the breath.

Listen to the man read. There are some recordings here and there, but for an era when everybody somehow found poetry interesting (in one small college five hundred crammed into a terrace to hear Ted Enslin read) there are relatively few recordings. Olson gave few public readings, powerful as they were. At the table or the shore, he would read to you when you were with him. Read loud and soft, full breath, at times as if he was smoking words or laughing them into place. What you heard is what "Projective Verse" insists on, breath of a human being being into words.

Works Cited

Allen, Donald, editor. *The New American Poetry, 1945-1960*. Grove Press, 1960.

Alcalay, Ammiel. *a little history*. Edited by Fred Dewey. re:public/UpSet Press, 2013.

Arendt, Hannah. *Between Past and Future*. 1961. Schocken Books, 1969.

_____. "Introduction." *Illuminations* by Walter Benjamin. Edited by Hannah Arendt. 1969. Schocken Books, 1978.

_____. *The Origins of Totalitarianism*. Harcourt Brace & Company, 1973.

Baudrillard, Jean. *America.*1969. Verso, 2020.

Bernstein, Charles. "Introjective Verse." *My Way: Speeches and Poems*. University of Chicago Press, 1999, 110-112.

Bey, Hakim. *T.A.Z. The Temporary Autonomous Zone, Ontological Anarchy, Poetic Terrorism*. Autonomedia, 1991.

Blaser, Robin. "The Violets: Charles Olson and Alfred North Whitehead." *The Fire: Collected Essays*. Edited by Miriam Nichols, University of California Press, 2006, 196-228.

Boughn, Michael. *Measure's Measures: Poetry and Knowledge*. Station Hill Press, 2024.

Boulus, Sargon. *"This Great River": Translating the Beats into Arabic*. Edited and translated by Khaled al-Hilli. Center for the Humanities at CUNY, 2024.

Charters, Ann. *T.S Eliot and Charles Olson—Young Tom and Charlie: Two American Poets at Home in Gloucester*. BW Walch Printing, 2024.

Clark, Tom. *Charles Olson: The Allegory of a Poet's Life*. W.W. Norton & Company, 1991.

Corbin, Henry. *Avicenna and the Visionary Recital.* Translated by Willard R. Trask, Bollingen Foundation, 1954.

_____. "Cyclic Time in Ismail Mazdaism and Ismailism." *Man and Time, Papers*

from the Eranos Yearbooks 3. Edited by Joseph Campbell, Princeton University Press, 1957.

_____. *Spiritual Body and Celestial Earth.* Translated by Nancy Pearson, Princeton University Press, 1989.

_____. *The Voyage and the Messenger: Iran and Philosophy.* North Atlantic Books, 1998.

Deleuze, Gilles. *Spinoza: Practical Philosophy*. Translated by Robert Hurley, City Lights, 1988.

Derrida, Jacques. *Of Grammatology.* Translated by Gayatri Chakravorty Spivak, Motilal Banarsidass, Johns Hopkins University Press, 1994.

Di Prima, Diane. *"Old Father, Old Artificer:" The Olson Memorial Lecture.* Edited by Ammiel Alcalay and Ana Božičević. Center for the Humanities at CUNY, 2012.

Dorn, Edward. *The Olson Memorial Lectures*. Edited by Lindsey M. Freer. Center for the Humanities at CUNY, 2012.

Duncan, Robert. *Charles Olson Memorial Lecture*. Edited by Ammiel Alcalay, Erica Kaufman, Meira Levinson, Bradley Lubin, Megan Paslawski, Kyle Waugh, and Rachael Wilson. Center for the Humanities at CUNY, 2011.

_____. *Imagining Persons: Robert Duncan's Lectures on Charles Olson*. Edited by Robert J. Bertholf and Dale M. Smith. University of New Mexico Press, 2017.

DuPlessis, Rachel Blau. *Purple Passages: Pound, Eliot, Zukofsky, Olson, Creeley, and the Ends of Patriarchal Poetry*. University of Iowa Press, 2012.

Foucault, Michel. *The Order of Things: An Archaeology of the Human Sciences.* 1966. Vintage, 1994.

Garcia, Edgar. *Signs of the Americas: A Poetics of Pictography, Hieroglyphs, and Khipu*. University of Chicago Press, 2020.

Grainger, Sam O'Hana. "Charles Olson: Psychological Warfare Executive." Chicago Review: https://www.chicagoreview.org/charles-olson-psychological-warfare-executive/ [accessed October 3, 2025].

Heidegger, Martin. *Being and Time.* Translated by John Macquarrie and Edward Robinson, Blackwell Publishers Ltd, 1962.

Herd, David. *Writing Against Expulsion in the Post-War World: Making Space for the Human*. Oxford University Press, 2023.

_____., editor. *Contemporary Olson.* University of Manchester Press, 2017.

Hoeynck, Joshua, editor. *Staying Open: Charles Olson's Sources and Influences.* Vernon Press, 2018.

Hollander, Benjamin, editor. *Letters to Olson.* Spuyten Duyvil, 2016.

Howe, Susan. "Since a Dialogue We Are." *Acts 10* (1989): 166-173.

Jung, C.G. *Aion: Researches into the Phenomenology of the Self* (Collected Works of C.G. Jung, Vol. 9, Part 2), Routledge, 1991.

Lacan, Jacques. *Ecrits: The First Complete English Language Edition.* Translated by Bruce Fink, W.W. Norton & Company, 2007.

Latour, Bruno. *How to Inhabit the Earth: Interviews with Nicolas Truong.* Translated by Julie Rose, Polity Press, 2024.

Mbembe, Achille. *Brutalism.* Translated by Steven Corcoran, Duke University Press, 2024.

Off, Carol. *At A Loss for Words: Conversation in the Age of Rage.* Random House Canada, 2024.

Olson, Charles. *Charles Olson and Frances Boldereff: A Modern Correspondence.* Edited by Ralph Maud and Sharon Thesen, Wesleyan University Press, 1999.

_____. and Frances Boldereff. *After Completion: The Later Letters.* Edited by Sharon Thesen. Talonbooks, 2012.

_____. *Causal Mythology*. Four Seasons Foundation, 1969.

_____. and Jeremy Prynne. *The Collected Letters of Charles Olson and Jeremy*

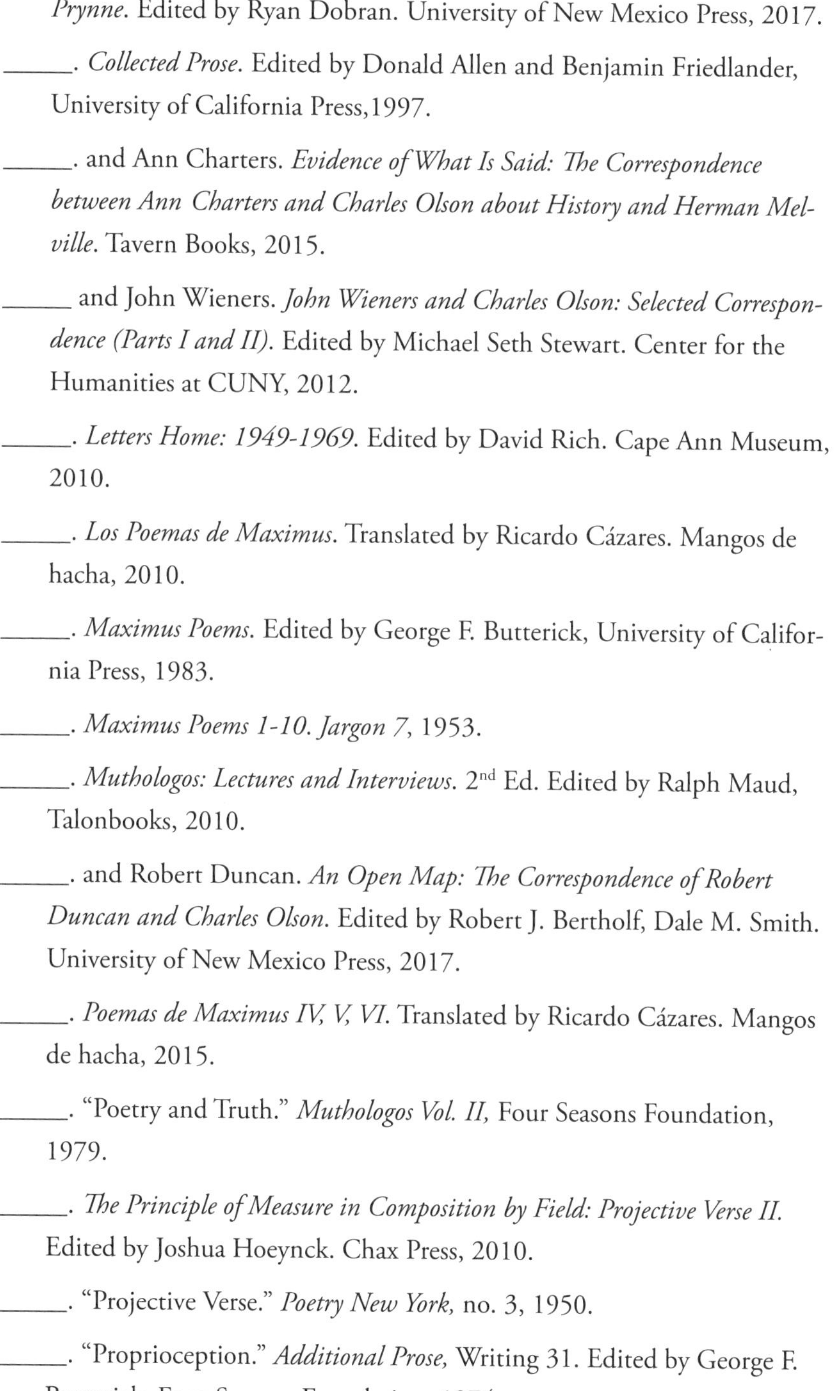

Prynne. Edited by Ryan Dobran. University of New Mexico Press, 2017.

_____. *Collected Prose*. Edited by Donald Allen and Benjamin Friedlander, University of California Press,1997.

_____. and Ann Charters. *Evidence of What Is Said: The Correspondence between Ann Charters and Charles Olson about History and Herman Melville*. Tavern Books, 2015.

_____ and John Wieners. *John Wieners and Charles Olson: Selected Correspondence (Parts I and II)*. Edited by Michael Seth Stewart. Center for the Humanities at CUNY, 2012.

_____. *Letters Home: 1949-1969*. Edited by David Rich. Cape Ann Museum, 2010.

_____. *Los Poemas de Maximus*. Translated by Ricardo Cázares. Mangos de hacha, 2010.

_____. *Maximus Poems*. Edited by George F. Butterick, University of California Press, 1983.

_____. *Maximus Poems 1-10. Jargon 7*, 1953.

_____. *Muthologos: Lectures and Interviews*. 2nd Ed. Edited by Ralph Maud, Talonbooks, 2010.

_____. and Robert Duncan. *An Open Map: The Correspondence of Robert Duncan and Charles Olson*. Edited by Robert J. Bertholf, Dale M. Smith. University of New Mexico Press, 2017.

_____. *Poemas de Maximus IV, V, VI*. Translated by Ricardo Cázares. Mangos de hacha, 2015.

_____. "Poetry and Truth." *Muthologos Vol. II,* Four Seasons Foundation, 1979.

_____. *The Principle of Measure in Composition by Field: Projective Verse II.* Edited by Joshua Hoeynck. Chax Press, 2010.

_____. "Projective Verse." *Poetry New York,* no. 3, 1950.

_____. "Proprioception." *Additional Prose,* Writing 31. Edited by George F. Butterick, Four Seasons Foundation, 1974.

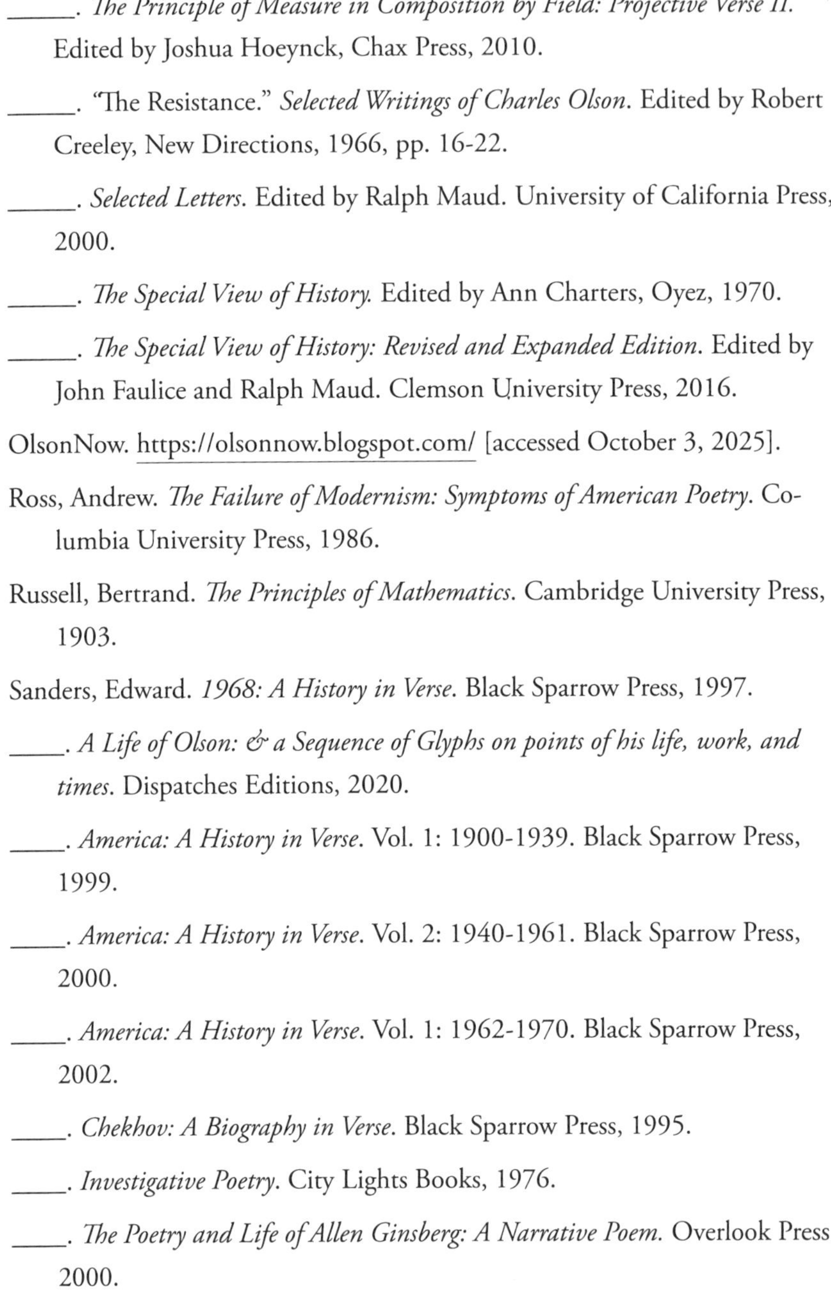

_____. *The Principle of Measure in Composition by Field: Projective Verse II.* Edited by Joshua Hoeynck, Chax Press, 2010.

_____. "The Resistance." *Selected Writings of Charles Olson*. Edited by Robert Creeley, New Directions, 1966, pp. 16-22.

_____. *Selected Letters*. Edited by Ralph Maud. University of California Press, 2000.

_____. *The Special View of History.* Edited by Ann Charters, Oyez, 1970.

_____. *The Special View of History: Revised and Expanded Edition*. Edited by John Faulice and Ralph Maud. Clemson University Press, 2016.

OlsonNow. https://olsonnow.blogspot.com/ [accessed October 3, 2025].

Ross, Andrew. *The Failure of Modernism: Symptoms of American Poetry*. Columbia University Press, 1986.

Russell, Bertrand. *The Principles of Mathematics*. Cambridge University Press, 1903.

Sanders, Edward. *1968: A History in Verse*. Black Sparrow Press, 1997.

____. *A Life of Olson: & a Sequence of Glyphs on points of his life, work, and times*. Dispatches Editions, 2020.

____. *America: A History in Verse*. Vol. 1: 1900-1939. Black Sparrow Press, 1999.

____. *America: A History in Verse*. Vol. 2: 1940-1961. Black Sparrow Press, 2000.

____. *America: A History in Verse*. Vol. 1: 1962-1970. Black Sparrow Press, 2002.

____. *Chekhov: A Biography in Verse*. Black Sparrow Press, 1995.

____. *Investigative Poetry*. City Lights Books, 1976.

____. *The Poetry and Life of Allen Ginsberg: A Narrative Poem.* Overlook Press, 2000.

Spears, André. "'Deep Time': Archeology and the Post-Romantic Paradigm." *Comparative Literature* (Autumn 1996): 343-358.

Stein, Charles. *The Secret of the Black Chrysanthemum: The Poetic Cosmology of Charles Olson & his use of the writings of C.G. Jung*. 1979. Station Hill Press, 1987.

Stein, Charles. "The Watch-House Where the Switches Keep." *The Critique of the Image is the Defense of the Imagination.* Autonomedia, 2020.

Stengers, Isabelle. *Making Sense in Common: A Reading of Whitehead in Times of Collapse*. Translated by Thomas Lamarre. University of Minnesota Press, 2023.

Stevens, Wallace. "Notes Toward a Supreme Fiction." *The Complete Poems of Wallace Stevens.* Vintage, 1990.

Taha, Aseel Abdul-Lateef. "Charles Olson's Historical Vision in 'The Kingfishers,'" Al-Adab Journal 11 (2015), 45-62. https://www.noormags.ir/view/en/articlepage/1238228/charles-olson-s-historical-vision-in-the-kingfishers. [Accessed October 3, 2025].

Tedlock, Dennis. *The Olson Codex: Projective Verse and the Problem of Mayan Hieroglyphics*. University of New Mexico Press, 2017.

Wiener, Norbert. *Cybernetics.* John Wiley & Sons, Inc., 1948.

____. *The Human Use of Human Beings: Cybernetics and Society.* Da Capo Press, 1988.

Whitehead, Alfred North. *Process and Reality: An Essay in Cosmology*. Macmillan, 1929.

Williams, William Carlos. *The Autobiography of William Carlos Williams.* New Directions, 1967.

Yépez, Heriberto. *The Empire of Neomemory*. Translated by Jen Hofer, Christian Nagler, Brian Whitener. ChainLinks, 2013.

Biographies

Ammiel Alcalay, poet, novelist, translator, critic, and scholar, is the author, co-author or translator of over thirty books, including *After Jews and Arabs: Remaking Levantine Culture*, *a little history*, *Memories of Our Future: Selected Essays, 1982-1999*, Semezdin Mehmedinović's *Sarajevo Blues*, and Faraj Bayrakdar's co-translated *A Dove in Free Flight*. Recent books include *CONTROLLED DEMOLITION: a work in four books*; the co-translation of Nasser Rabah's *Gaza: The Poem Said Its Piece*; and a book of essays, *Follow the Person: Archival Encounters*. A new book of poems, *Imperial Abhorrences / For Palestine*, in collaboration with the Palestinian artist Kholoud Hammad, is forthcoming. While bringing works from other parts of the world to the US via translation and advocacy, Alcalay has helped reconfigure contemporary US literary and cultural history through his publishing, pedagogical, and public project, *Lost & Found: The CUNY Poetics Document Initiative*, recognized in 2017 with a Before Columbus Foundation American Book Award. At Queens College, CUNY, he is former chair of the Department of Classical, Middle Eastern & Asian Languages & Cultures, and teaches in the MFA in Creative Writing and Literary Translation. At the CUNY Graduate Center, Alcalay is a member of various faculties. He was named Distinguished Professor in 2023.

Michael Boughn is the author of *Measure's Measures—Poetry and Knowledge* (Station Hill, 2024), and several books of poetry, including *Cosmographia—A Post-Lucretian Faux Micro-Epic*, *Hermetic Divagations—After H.D.*, *City—A Poem from the End of the World*, and *The Book of Uncertain—A Hyperbiographical User's Manual, Books 1 & 2*. He was co-editor of Robert Duncan's *The H.D. Book,* and from 2016 to 2020 together with Kent Johnson produced the online Temporary Autonomous Zone known as *Dispatches from the Poetry Wars.*

Robert Kelly was born in 1935 in Brooklyn. He has published scores of books of poetry, fiction, and essays. He has taught at many universities, but mostly, and for 60 years, at Bard College. His most recent books are the collection *Linden Word*, the experimental series *Listening Through*, and *Symphonies*. A new collection, *Metalogues*, is forthcoming from Station Hill. He lives in the Hudson Valley with his wife, the French translator Charlotte Mandell.

Miriam Nichols is Professor Emerita in the Department of English at the University of the Fraser Valley where she taught literary theory, Canadian and American literature, and international modernism. Her publications include scholarly editions of the poet Robin Blaser's *The Fire: Collected Essays* and *The Holy Forest: Collected Poems* (University of California Press, 2006) and *The Astonishment Tapes* (University of Alabama, 2015). She is the author of *Radical Affections: Essays on the Poetics of Outside* (Alabama, 2010) and *A Literary Biography of Robin Blaser: Mechanic of Splendor* (Palgrave, 2019). She currently works for Harbour Publishing in Madeira Park on the Sunshine Coast of B.C.

George Quasha, poet, artist, and writer explores certain principles (e.g., *axiality, ecoproprioception*) in various mediums. His unexampled genre *preverbs*, begun 2001, in serial books includes *Things Done for Themselves* (Marsh Hawk, 2015), *Not Even Rabbits Go Down This Hole* (Spuyten Duyvil, 2020) , *Waking from Myself* (Station Hill, 2022) and *Hearing Other* (Chax, 2025). Other books include *Poetry in Principle: Essays in Poetics* (foreword Edward Casey, Spuyten Duyvil, 2019), *Axial Stones: An Art of Precarious Balance* (foreword Carter Ratcliff, North Atlantic Books, 2006), *An Art of Limina: Gary Hill's Works & Writings* (with Charles Stein, foreword Lynne Cooke, Ediciones Polígrafa, 2009) and *art is (Speaking Portraits)* (PAJ, 2016). His work is discussed in *Zero Point Poiesis: George Quasha's Axial Art* (Aporeia, 2022) edited Burt Kimmelman, foreword Jerome McGann. His anthologies include

America a Prophecy: A New Reading of American Poetry from Pre-Colombian Times to the Present (with Jerome Rothenberg, Random House, 1973; Station Hill, 2012). A Guggenheim Fellow, NEA Fellow, and recipient of the T-Space poetry award, he collaborates on work with artist Susan Quasha, with whom he is also co-publisher of Station Hill Press in Barrytown, NY.

Ed Sanders left Kansas City, Missouri for New York City in 1958, and was in jail (for the first time, but not the last) by 1961 for opposing the launch of nuclear armed submarines. Among other things, he went on to write "A Poem from Jail," open an essential bookstore (Peace Eye), launch a ground-breaking mimeo magazine, *Fuck You, A Magazine of the Arts*, found the still performing proto-punk rock band, The Fugs, write the definitive book on Charles Manson and his "family", found the Investigative Poetry movement, write a history of USAmerica in verse, help levitate the Pentagon in protest against the war against Viet Nam, and write the definitive biography (in glyphs) of Charles Olson. Among other things.

In recognition of his work, Sanders has been awarded a Guggenheim Fellowship, an NEA Fellowship, the American Book Award, and an Award from the Foundation for Contemporary Arts. He lives in Woodstock, NY with his wife, writer and artist Miriam Sanders.

Charles Stein's work comprises a complexly integrated field of poems, prose reflections, translations, drawings, photographs, lectures, conversations, and performances. Born 1944 in New York City, he is the author of thirteen books of poetry including *From Mimir's Head: Poems from theforestforthetrees (1994-2000)* (Station Hill, 2011) and *Black Light Casts White Shadows* (Lunar Chandelier Collective, 2018). He is the author of a critical study of Charles Olson's use of the writing of C.G. Jung, *The Secret of the Black Chrysanthemum* (Station Hill, 1987); *Persephone Unveiled* (North Atlantic Books, 2006); *The Light of Hermes Trismegistus: New Translations of Seven Essential Hermetic Texts* (Inner

Traditions, 2022); and verse translation of *The Iliad* (North Atlantic Books) and *The Odyssey* (forthcoming). He holds a Ph.D. in literature from the University of Connecticut at Storrs and lives with guitarist, choral director, and research historian Megan Hastie in Barrytown, NY. His work can be sampled at his website: www.charlessteinpoet.co.